A Chicken in Every Pot

Edith Vanocur

THOMAS Y. CROWELL COMPANY
ESTABLISHED 1834   NEW YORK

Copyright © 1976 by Sander Vanocur

Designed by Abigail Moseley

Manufactured in the United States of America

Library of Congress Cataloging in Publication Data

A Chicken in every pot.

    Includes index.
    1.   Cookery (Chicken)   I.   Vanocur, Edith.
TX750.C45   641.6′6′5   75-46581
ISBN 0-690-00391-9

1 2 3 4 5 6 7 8 9 10

For Nick and Chris

ACKNOWLEDGMENTS

Edith had finished nearly all the writing of this book before she began a long and painful struggle against the cancer which finally ended her life.

My sons and I would like to express our gratitude to the following for helping to complete the work she had begun: Margaret Miner, Susan Arensberg, Peg Schreiber, and Sharon Armann.

Our thanks also to Ben Bradlee and *The Washington Post* for permitting the reproduction of many of the recipes which first appeared in that newspaper.

—SANDER VANOCUR

CONTENTS

INTRODUCTION

MEMORIES AND BASICS

A lot of jokes have been made at the expense of the Jewish mother and her way with chicken soup and the many other things she does with chickens. For once I am willing to gamble: I'd see anyone's Jewish mother and raise them mine when it comes to using all of a chicken.

Let me explain. The chicken of my childhood in Vienna came with white feathers and bright-yellow legs. First we would pluck the chicken, and when we'd collected enough feathers, we'd make them into feather-beds (inferior ones, it's true, since the good ones were made of goose down). Then the chicken was drawn, and after the unwanted insides were thrown away, what was left was a lot of good chicken fat, unborn eggs, a chicken liver, stomach, and heart. The neck was chopped off, and the longer it was, the better, since the skin made a casing for forcemeat sausage.

The fat was rendered over slow heat. It was then spread on garlic toast or used for cooking: it was one of the ingredients for making chopped liver and was the base for sauces and gravies. The fibers that were left, almost fatless, in the rendering pan were called *Grammel.* Unfortunately, there was only a spoonful or so of those. Heavily salted, they made a magnificent snack.

The chicken liver was fought over by the different factions of the family. Some wanted chopped liver; others wanted the liver sautéed in some of the chicken fat with the unborn eggs; and almost everyone wanted it included in the stuffing for the neck skin. One little liver and so many uses!

The chicken feet, the first joint of the wings, and the skinless neck were simmered with an onion and a veal knuckle for soup or a sauce if the bird was to be roasted. But more often than not the "roaster" also landed in the soup pot for a little while to enrich the soup.

After the chicken was eaten, the leftover carcass, of course, was put in the stock pot for further use, forming the base for more soups or aspics. The unborn eggs, if they lasted this long, were poached at the last moment in such a soup. So, for every part of a chicken there were several uses.

I was also raised long enough ago to remember that among many other delights spring meant delicacies on the table that appeared at no other time of the year. A whole roasted kid was one. And at Easter we had lamb, no larger than the turkey we buy now. But best of all was spring chicken frying in bread crumbs. It was a very distinct smell, since the chicken was always fried in rendered pork fat.

Spring chicken was something to look forward to all year long and to look back on when summer came and the chickens were too large to be just fried. The first indication of that came when the chicken pieces were parboiled before frying to make them tender, much as a woman might use more makeup or dye her hair when she feels she's no longer a "spring chicken."

The size of that spring chicken then resembled that of the broiler now. These broilers, as well as the slightly larger fryer, have one advantage over the spring chicken of long ago: they are available year round. They are also still more economical to buy per pound than meat, and because the flesh of young chickens is the most easily assimilated of animal food, it makes it a particularly good general diet.

Unfortunately, that "general diet" chicken is lacking in taste. It is no longer possible to let the cockerel or hen scratch around the barnyard and dig up worms, seeds, and natural sources of antibiotics. In the race to get the heaviest bird in the shortest time with the best pigmentation to meet the increasing demand, chickens are now bred on various feeds, plus hormone additives and antibiotics. So it is better to know where your chicken was raised or if it was inspected. For those interested in feed tables and other specifics, the United States Department of Agriculture Handbook No. 320, *Commercial Broiler Production*, is an excellent study in raising meat birds. It is invaluable to the chicken farmer, if somewhat alarming to the consumer, because it answers questions some of us have not learned yet to ask.

The roasting hen and the stewing chicken have more of a chance to taste better than the smaller fryer or broiler. Having survived the conditions of stress, hormones, and antibiotics and lived beyond the eight weeks it takes to raise the "spring chicken," there is a possibility that such a hen will be fattened on corn or even some form of wheat. Both make a great deal of difference to the taste of the bird.

It is of little use to say at this point how to tell a roaster from a stewer, since most chickens come to us cleaned, wrapped in plastic, and often frozen. On a fresh chicken there is one way left to differentiate a large hen from an old fowl. Bend the end of the breastbone opposite the wishbone. If it bends, you have a roaster; if it snaps, you have an old hen for stewing.

CHICKEN NOTES

YIELD

A 5-pound stewing chicken yields 2 pounds of cooked meat.

About 2-1/2 pounds of chicken breasts yield 1 pound of meat, boned.

1 pound of chicken will yield 1 cup of meat.

CHOLESTEROL

No meat is lower in fat content—64 percent of the fatty acids in chicken is unsaturated.

CALORIES

A 3-ounce, skinless, broiled chicken breast has 115 calories. If the skin is still on, it has 185 calories.

STORING

Remember that the chicken in your supermarket was wrapped for sale, not storage. To store, remove the store wrapping, rinse, dry thoroughly, rewrap, and store in the coldest part of the refrigerator. Most chicken should be frozen after 2 days if you're going to keep the meat longer (that is, if it wasn't frozen before you bought it).

FREEZING

Uncooked poultry should not be frozen longer than 3 months.

Cooked poultry, frozen in broth, should not be kept longer than 6 months; without broth, only 1 month.

All poultry must be wrapped in airtight, moisture-resistant material before freezing. Never freeze or refrigerate a stuffed chicken. Once it is stuffed, it must be cooked at once.

THAWING

It is best to thaw chickens in the refrigerator. Allow 1 to 2 days for a large chicken (over 4 pounds). Allow 12 to 16 hours for a small chicken (less than 4 pounds).

A chicken will take approximately 2 hours per pound to defrost at room temperature.

TO POACH OR BRAISE A CHICKEN

When food is cooked in liquid, much of its taste and nutrients inevitably pass into this liquid. At the outset, one must decide where the flavor should end up. If a chicken is to be used for salads, or made into a dish with just a little sauce, and the flavor and nutrient are to be preserved in the solid as much as possible, it should be braised or steamed. If the chicken is to be made into soup or aspic, where it is important to have most of the flavor in the liquid, it should be boiled or poached.

The difference between steaming or braising and poaching or boiling is the amount of liquid in the pot. For steaming only a minute amount of water is used and most of the chicken will be cooked by steam or it will be elevated, not touching the boiling liquid, and all of the chicken will be cooked by steam only. Braising starts with no liquid but lots of seasonings, thus flavoring the natural juices. Water may be added later.

For poaching or boiling, most or all of the chicken will be submerged in liquid. The difference between poaching and boiling is in the temperature. Poaching suggests a lower temperature than boiling. In either case, the chicken should be started in cold water, which should be brought to a boil as slowly as possible. This will break down the connecting fibers most effectively and allow free flow of flavor and nutrients into the liquid. As a matter of fact, the longer and slower the cooking, the better chicken stock you will get. If, in the following recipes, I have not always followed this rule it is because of the many uses I find for leftover liquid or leftover chicken. And certainly I've used the meat of a boiled or poached chicken, or added bones and more water to the little liquid left over from a braised chicken to make stock.

POACHED CHICKEN

For meat, then stock.

1 stewing or roasting chicken, 5 to 6 pounds
1 onion, peeled and halved
2 stalks celery, cut up
Several sprigs parsley
2 carrots, cut up
2 or 3 cloves garlic, peeled and halved
Salt and pepper or peppercorns
Enough cold water to cover a little more than half the chicken

Place all the ingredients in a stewing kettle. Cover and simmer very gently until the fowl is done. The time will depend on the age of the bird. Insert a skewer or fork in the thickest part of the thigh: if the juices run clear, the fowl is done; if the juices run pink, it is not. Cool the chicken in the broth, then remove.

After the meat has been removed, the carcass of the chicken can be put back in the broth, and more water added. Further slow simmering, uncovered, will make excellent chicken stock.

Chicken stock may be strained, cooled, and then refrigerated for 3 to 4 days or frozen for weeks. Leave the fat on as a seal, and remove it before using the stock itself.

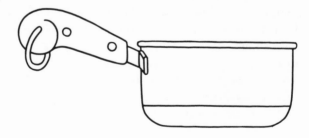

BRAISED CHICKEN

For good cooked meat.

1 stalk celery, halved
4 sprigs parsley
1 sprig thyme
1 bay leaf
4 to 6 thick slices bacon, or a
  piece of skin from a ham

1 large stewing or roasting
  chicken, seasoned with salt
  and pepper
1 lemon, sliced
2 or 3 onions or leeks
2 or 3 carrots
A paste made of flour and water

Tie together with natural string the celery, parsley, thyme, and bay leaf—the *bouquet garni*.

Line a heavy casserole or Dutch oven, one with a well-fitting lid, with the bacon or ham skin—this will prevent the chicken from touching the bottom of the pan and burning. Put in the chicken and cover the breast with slices of lemon. Add the *bouquet garni*, onions or leeks, and carrots, then seal the lid shut with the flour paste. Set the pan over very low heat.

Uncover after 45 minutes and look inside the pot; decide if you will need more liquid than the natural juices, and, if so, add a little water and estimate how much longer the chicken will need to cook. Cover again, and weigh down the lid. Cook until the juices run clear, not pink, when a fork is inserted in the thickest part of the thigh. Discard the *bouquet garni* and skim the excess fat off the juices.

Soups

These recipes call for good chicken stock, which means you should really make your own (see the section on poaching a chicken, with the sample recipe on page 6). If you get into the habit of making and saving stock whenever the opportunity arises, you'll have it on hand when you suddenly want to make the Basic Cream of Chicken Soup, or a tart lemon soup, or the substantial Spanish Chicken Soup, or the elegant cold Senegalese Soup . . . .

COCK-A-LEEKIE

Serves 8

2 bunches leeks
2 tablespoons butter
1 small chicken, whole or cut up

9 cups good veal or chicken stock, well seasoned
2 tablespoons raw rice or barley

Clean the leeks well and slice into 1-inch rings, using all the white and as much of the green as possible. Sauté in a skillet in the melted butter until tender but not brown, stirring often. Remove with a slotted spoon and drain on paper towels. Add the chicken to the skillet and brown evenly until barely brown.

Transfer the chicken to a soup kettle. Add the reserved leeks and stock and simmer, covered, until the chicken is almost tender. Add the rice or barley and continue to cook until the rice or barley and the chicken are cooked. The meat from the chicken can be removed from the carcass before serving, or serve each person with a piece of chicken and some of the soup.

BASIC CREAM OF CHICKEN SOUP

Serves 4

3 tablespoons butter	Salt and a generous helping of
1/4 cup all-purpose flour	freshly ground white pepper
5 cups good chicken stock	1/2 cup heavy cream

Melt the butter in a saucepan over low heat and add the flour. Stirring constantly, cook the roux for 2 or 3 minutes. Stir in the stock with a balloon whisk, a little at a time. Cook the soup, stirring constantly, until it's completely smooth—about 10 minutes, or longer if you like a very thick soup. Season to taste.

Just before serving, turn off the heat and add the cream. The soup may be reheated, but it must not boil after the addition of the cream.

VARIATIONS

1. Serve the above soup with diced smoked tongue to decorate.
2. Add 1 or 2 teaspoons of curry powder to the roux.

AVGOLEMONO

This is the famous Greek lemon soup.

Serves 6

8 to 9 cups good chicken stock	4 large eggs
1 cup raw rice	6 tablespoons lemon juice
Salt and pepper	Chopped parsley or dill

Bring the stock to a boil. Add the rice and simmer for 15 minutes, until the rice is soft. Add salt and pepper to taste, and leave the soup simmering.

Beat the eggs until very light and frothy—about 5 minutes. Add the lemon juice slowly and continue to beat. Very slowly add 1 cup of the simmering soup to the eggs while still beating them. Then turn the heat off under the soup and pour the egg mixture into it, stirring—otherwise the eggs will curdle. Serve decorated with parsley or dill.

HOT LEMON SOUP

Here is another good lemon soup, with a touch of garlic and hot sauce, and dollops of whipped cream on top.

Serves 6 to 8

6 cups good chicken stock
6 sprigs parsley
2 cloves garlic, peeled and
    pierced
1 slice onion
1 teaspoon grated lemon rind
3 tablespoons olive or safflower
    seed oil

1/8 teaspoon hot sauce
3 tablespoons fresh lemon
    juice, or more to taste
2 egg yolks
6 to 8 teaspoons whipped cream

Bring the stock to a boil with the parsley, garlic, onion, lemon rind, and 1 tablespoon of the oil. Simmer, uncovered, for 20 minutes over low heat. Strain and discard the solids.

Add the hot sauce and lemon juice to the soup. Beat the egg yolks until light in color. Continue to beat while adding the 2 remaining tablespoons of oil.

To serve, bring the soup to the boiling point, then remove from the heat. While stirring dribble the egg mixture in slowly to prevent curdling. Serve in preheated cups, with about 1 teaspoon of whipped cream floating on top.

SOUP SENEGALESE

A wonderful cold puréed soup flavored with curry and cream.

Serves 4

1 red onion, chopped
2 chicken breast halves, skinned and boned
2 tablespoons butter
A few drops dark sesame oil (optional)

2 tablespoons curry powder
3 tablespoons instant-blending flour
Salt and freshly ground pepper
4 cups good chicken stock, hot
1 cup Half and Half

Sauté the onion and chicken in the butter and oil until both are cooked—about 10 minutes. Add the curry powder and flour and season to taste. Cook for 3 minutes more, without browning, stirring constantly. Cube the chicken and add, with onions, to some stock in a blender and blend until smooth, stirring in the rest of the stock after the chicken and onions are well blended. Chill thoroughly. Just before serving, stir in the chilled cream.

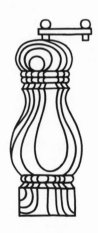

CHINESE HOT CHICKEN AND EGG SOUP

A good stock is laced with colorful shredded ingredients.

Serves 6

6 cups good chicken stock
A few drops dark sesame oil
1 hot green Chinese pepper,
    minced; OR 1/2 teaspoon
    Korean bean mash (both are
    very hot)
1 large chicken breast, skinned,
    boned, and shredded
1 cup parboiled and rinsed rice
    sticks

2 cups fresh bean sprouts,
    rinsed and dried
6 whole scallions, cut into
    3-inch pieces and shredded
    lengthwise
1 teaspoon soy sauce
3 eggs, beaten

Bring the stock to a boil and turn the heat down to "simmer." Add the sesame oil and green pepper or bean mash. Add the shredded chicken—it will only take about 5 minutes to cook; do not overcook.

Turn the heat high and add the rice sticks, the bean sprouts, shredded scallions, and soy sauce. As soon as the soup boils again, turn off the heat and pour in the eggs in a circular motion, stirring gently. The eggs will separate into shreds (they are often referred to as "egg petals"). Serve immediately in small bowls with porcelain spoons.

SPANISH CHICKEN SOUP

A hearty soup of vegetables, chicken, rice, and hot sausage.

Serves 6

8 cups good chicken stock
2 or 3 potatoes, peeled and
   sliced
1 turnip, peeled and sliced
1 large red onion, roughly
   chopped
3 cloves garlic, peeled and
   crushed
3 stalks celery, chopped

3 carrots, scraped and sliced
1/2 cup raw long-grain rice
1/2 pound, or more, Spanish
   chorizo sausage, sliced
1 cup bits of cooked chicken
   meat
Salt and pepper to taste
1 teaspoon crushed cumin seed
   (optional)

Bring the chicken stock to a boil. Add the potatoes, turnip, onion, garlic, celery, and carrots. Cover the pan and simmer the soup for 15 minutes. Add the rice, sausage, and chicken meat. Cover and simmer the soup for 20 minutes more, or until the rice is done. Season and serve.

NOTE: *Chorizo* sausages are highly seasoned, so season the soup after the sausages have been cooked.

ITALIAN CHICKEN SOUP WITH EGGS AND SPINACH

Serves 4

1 fryer, 2-1/2 to 3 pounds	1 tablespoon seasoned salt
1 packet soup bones	The peel of 1 lemon
1 medium onion, whole	1 pound fresh spinach, stems
2 carrots, whole	removed
2 stalks celery or half a celery	3 eggs
root	1/4 cup grated Parmesan
6 peppercorns	

Put all the ingredients except the spinach, eggs, and cheese in a kettle and cover with cold water. Bring to a boil as slowly as possible and skim. Simmer for about 50 minutes to 1 hour, or until the chicken is done. Strain and skim as much of the fat from the top of the broth as possible. Correct the seasoning.

Clean the spinach and cook for 3 or 4 minutes in a small amount of boiling water. Strain and chop the spinach in a colander, then, with the back of a spoon, press as much of the liquid from the spinach as possible. Keep it warm while you beat the eggs lightly. Bring the soup to a boil, and while beating it add the eggs all at once. Boil for 2 minutes longer. To serve, add some spinach to each plate of soup and sprinkle with Parmesan cheese. You could serve pieces of the chicken in the soup or carve and serve it separately (or use it later).

JAPANESE CLEAR CHICKEN SOUP

Serves 2

2 chicken legs, each chopped
  into 4 pieces
5 cups water
1/2 pound *daikon* (Japanese
  radish), cut into 1-inch
  pieces

1 or 2 carrots, scraped and cut
  into 1-inch pieces
3 tablespoons sake
1 tablespoon soy sauce
Salt, if necessary
1 whole scallion, minced

Cook the chicken legs in the water over low heat until very tender, skimming off the fat during the cooking. Add the *daikon*, carrots, sake, soy sauce, and salt to taste. Cook over high heat so the soup reduces to 2 cups and the vegetables stay crisp. Serve garnished with the minced scallion.

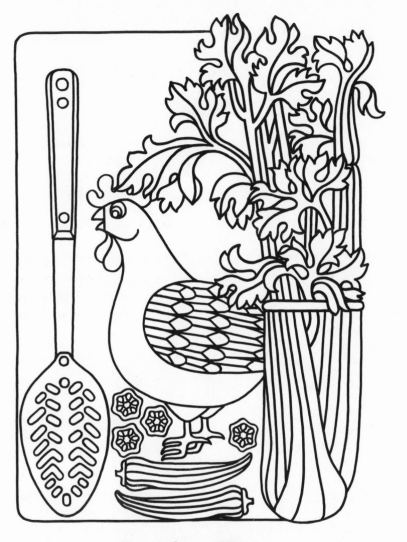

In the Pot

CASSEROLED

"In the pot" chicken is casseroled chicken, whether, as arranged here, whole, in pieces, or boned. The recipes in this chapter generally reflect the method of browning first, then transferring to a casserole with other ingredients for a slow cooking, mostly on top of the stove. And though there are some "oven-roasted" casseroles, the lid makes all the difference—when it's on, the process isn't true roasting.

Certainly there is some overlap here with browned chicken that's then simmered in a covered skillet, but the casserole's the key here, plus the quantity and variety of ingredients.

So, here are some long-simmered chickens, with cranberries, or white wine, or garlic, or such meals in themselves as Chicken Gumbo, Chicken Pie, or West Indian Pepper Pot. . . .

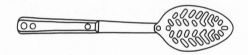

WHOLE CHICKEN

CHICKEN BAKED IN SALT

The Chinese do this in a wok on top of the stove. Here you do it in a covered casserole—very simple, and the chicken is wonderfully moist with its own juices. It is not salty. The skin, with its tight smoothness, just faintly tastes of salt.

Serves 2 or 3

1 whole fryer   3 to 5 pounds coarse salt (such
                                        as kosher salt)

Bring the chicken to room temperature and dry it well. Select a casserole with a cover, about 1 or 2 inches larger than the chicken, and fill it two-thirds full of salt. Put some additional salt in another casserole and bake the salt in both casseroles at 425 degrees for 30 minutes, stirring at times. Then scoop out some of the salt from the casserole you want to bake with, place the chicken in the scooped-out place, and cover with the remaining hot salt. Bake at 400 degrees, covered, for 1-1/4 hours.

Lift the chicken from the casserole, and if necessary wipe adhering salt off the chicken with a damp paper towel. This chicken will not taste salty if the salt was hot to start with. Serve hot or cold.

CHICKEN BAKED IN CIDER

A beautifully simple recipe—chicken roasted in a covered casserole with apples and cider.

Serves 2 or 3

1 whole fryer
Salt and pepper
2 medium-sized onions, peeled
4 tart apples, peeled and
    quartered

1/4 cup Calvados (optional)
1 6-ounce can frozen cider
    concentrate

Season the chicken inside and out. Place the onions in the cavity of the chicken. Place the apples in the bottom of a casserole and the chicken on top of the apples. Mix the Calvados and cider and pour over the chicken.

Cover the casserole tightly and bake at 400 degrees for 1 hour or less, until tender but not quite "done." Baste once or twice during baking. Uncover and bake 10 more minutes, basting frequently. The sugar in the liquids will glaze the chicken a beautiful brown.

POULET RÔTI EN CASSEROLE

A classic casserole-roasted chicken—encased in tarragon-flavored butter, roasted with vegetables, then the juices glazed with wine to make a wonderful light sauce.

Serves 4

Select a casserole that is only just large enough to hold the chicken, that has a well-fitting lid, and that can be used on top of the stove as well as in the oven.

The chicken should be trussed if it is to be carved at the table. (See page 75.)

1 roasting chicken, about 4 pounds, trussed, at room temperature

2 cloves garlic, peeled and halved

1/2 cup cooking oil plus 2 tablespoons butter

1 stick (1/4 pound) butter, softened

8 sprigs (or more) fresh tarragon

20 pearl onions, peeled

16 small carrots, scraped

1-1/2 cups dry white wine or champagne

Beurre manié: 1-1/2 tablespoons all-purpose flour mixed with 1-1/2 tablespoons softened butter

Salt and pepper

Pat the chicken dry. Rub it well with garlic and slip the remaining garlic inside the cavity. In a flameproof casserole or Dutch oven heat the oil with the 2 tablespoons butter. Brown the chicken on all sides, turning often. When the chicken is golden brown, lift it onto a platter to cool. Discard the fat, leaving the particles on the bottom unless they are burned.

Make a "beauty paste" of the stick of softened butter and 4 sprigs or more of tarragon, chopped. Rub the paste over the entire chicken and place it in the casserole or Dutch oven and bake, covered, at 325 to 350 degrees for 1-1/2 hours, or until the chicken is done. Baste at times.

Half an hour or so before the end of the cooking time, add the onions and carrots to the casserole. Turn the vegetables at least once during cooking.

When the chicken and vegetables are done, transfer them to a platter and keep warm. Drain the sauce of excess fat and over medium heat deglaze with white wine, stirring constantly with a wire whisk. Add the *beurre manié* bit by bit, stirring, until the sauce is as thick as you like it. Simmer until the flour no longer tastes raw, about 2 minutes. Season. Blanch the remaining sprigs of tarragon in the sauce for 1 minute. Pour the sauce over the chicken and decorate with blanched sprigs of tarragon.

SPANISH CHICKEN WITH SAUCE

This rice-and-sausage-stuffed chicken has a spicy tomato sauce as an accompaniment.

Serves 4 to 6

1-1/2 cups Spanish or Polish sausage, diced	1 roasting chicken, 4 pounds or more
1-1/2 cups cooked saffron rice	1/4 cup oil
1 bunch whole scallions, chopped	2 tablespoons butter
Salt, if necessary	1/2 cup dry white wine
	Tomato Sauce (see page 25)

Combine the sausage, rice, and scallions. Add salt if necessary. Truss and stuff the chicken with this mixture (see pages 75-77). In a heavy casserole or Dutch oven, combine and heat the oil and butter. Brown the chicken on all sides. Add the wine, cover the casserole and simmer over low heat until the chicken is done—about 1-1/4 hours.

While the chicken is cooking, start the sauce.

Lift the chicken from the kettle when it is done and keep it warm. Discard excess fat from the kettle and deglaze over medium heat with the wine, scraping and stirring. (This is for the sauce.) Reheat the sauce and serve with the chicken.

TOMATO SAUCE

1/4 cup oil
1 very large red onion, peeled and sliced
1 pound tomatoes, peeled and chopped
2 tablespoons tomato paste
1 tablespoon granulated sugar

2 tablespoons Dijon-style mustard
1 tablespoon sweet Hungarian paprika
1/2 to 1 cup dry white wine glaze
Salt

Heat the oil in a large skillet and sauté the onion over very low heat without browning until tender—about 10 minutes; stir often. Add the tomatoes and continue to cook and stir. When the tomatoes are done (about 10 minutes), add the tomato paste, sugar, mustard, and paprika. Just before serving, add the wine glaze and salt.

POT AU FEU

A delicious "big" dish—simmered beef and bones, a whole simmered chicken, some sausage, lots of vegetables.

Serves 8

3 or 4 beef shin bones, with as much lean meat as possible, about 3 pounds
1 marrow bone, cut in pieces, or a veal knuckle
1 large onion, peeled and sliced
About 6 leeks, trimmed and cleaned
8 carrots, scraped
8 stalks celery
1 stewing chicken, about 5 pounds
2 cloves garlic, minced
Salt and pepper
2 Polish ring sausages
1 package tiny frozen peas
1 package frozen Chinese snow peas or 1/2 pound fresh ones

Place the marrow bone, the shin bones, and lean beef in a large kettle. Add enough water to cover the meat by an inch. Add the onion and bring to a boil, skim, and simmer, covered, for 2 hours. Add half the leeks, 4 carrots, and 4 celery stalks; season and continue simmering until meat and vegetables test done—about 30 minutes. Leaving the meat in the kettle, remove the bones and discard.

About 1 hour after putting the beef on to boil, place the chicken in a small flameproof casserole. Add the remaining leeks, carrots, celery, garlic, salt, and pepper. Add enough water to cover the dark meat of the chicken—this way the white meat will be steam-cooked. (It may be necessary to add more water as the cooking progresses.) Bring to a boil and simmer, covered, until chicken is done, approximately 1-1/2 hours.

About 1 hour after starting the chicken, place the sausage in a pan with enough water to cover. Bring to a boil and simmer for 20 to 30 minutes. Strain and discard the water.

Add the sausages to the boiled beef. When the chicken is ready, combine the chicken and chicken broth with the beef and beef broth and the sausages. Boil together only long enough to add and cook the peas and pea pods, about 5 minutes.

POULET AU RIZ

A lightly flavored, simmered chicken, with pearl onions and rice.

Serves 4 to 6

1 1-inch-square piece of salt
   pork or slab bacon
1 stewing chicken,
   about 5 pounds
5 cups water
1 *bouquet garni*: about 2 sprigs
   parsley, 1/2 bay leaf, 1 sprig
   or 1/8 teaspoon thyme,
   wrapped in cheesecloth

Salt and pepper
1/2 teaspoon ground mace
16 pearl onions, peeled
2 cups raw rice

Place the pork or bacon in a large kettle and fry for a minute or so on each side. Remove it from the pan and reserve. Brown the hen in the rendered fat as evenly as possible on all sides, then discard all the fat from the kettle. Add to the chicken the reserved pork or bacon, water, and *bouquet garni*, and season with salt and pepper. (It should be oversalted, since the rice will balance the saltiness.) Cover and simmer for 30 minutes.

Discard the *bouquet garni* and add the mace and pearl onions. Continue to simmer until the hen is cooked but not overdone. Remove the chicken from the kettle and measure the liquid. It should now be 4 cups or just under. Return this amount to the kettle and add the rice. Place the chicken on top of the rice, cover, and simmer for 20 minutes, or until the rice and chicken are cooked.

WEST INDIAN PEPPER POT

Chicken simmered, then lamb, pork, stewing vegetables, and shrimp added—a meal all by itself.

Serves 6 to 8

1 veal knuckle
1 large stewing chicken, 4 to 5
    pounds
1 or 2 fresh hot red peppers,
    seeded and chopped
1 teaspoon peppercorns
1/2 pound lean fresh pork or
    1/2-inch ham slices
1/2 pound lean lamb, cut up
4 medium-sized onions
4 medium-sized potatoes

4 large carrots
2 white turnips
8 sprigs parsley
1 bay leaf
1 small cabbage, cut into
    wedges
1 cup fresh spinach leaves
1 cup shelled shrimp (optional)
Salt and cayenne pepper to
    taste

Put the veal knuckle and stewing hen in a very large kettle. Cover with cold water, add the pepper and peppercorns, and bring to a boil as slowly as possible, skimming as necessary. Cover and simmer while you prepare the other ingredients.

Meanwhile, cook the pork or ham in a dry skillet until golden on all sides. Remove with a slotted spoon, drain on paper towels, and reserve. Brown the lamb in the same skillet, drain, and reserve with the pork.

Peel the onions, potatoes, carrots, and turnips and add them, whole, to the hen; add the parsley and bay leaf. Simmer the chicken and vegetables for about 1 hour, then add the reserved meats and cabbage. Cook for about 15 to 20 minutes. Add the shrimp and spinach and cook only a few more minutes. Season with salt and cayenne pepper—as the name suggests, this dish should be peppery hot.

CHICKEN PIE

A whole simmered chicken is then baked with leeks and sausages under a pie crust. Vermouth flavors the stock in the pie.

Serves 4 to 6

1 whole stewing chicken, about 4 pounds
1 cup cooking oil
Water to cover about half the chicken
1 *bouquet garni*: about 2 sprigs parsley, 1/2 bay leaf, 1 sprig or 1/8 teaspoon thyme, wrapped in cheesecloth
2 onions, peeled
2 carrots
2 stalks celery
Salt and pepper

4 to 6 slices bacon, in 1-inch pieces
1 pound garlic sausage, Spanish or Polish, sliced in 1/2-inch rings
Chicken Pie Crust or Alternate Crust (see page 30)
1 to 2 bunches leeks, washed and trimmed, cut into 2-inch rings
1/4 cup chopped parsley
1 cup dry vermouth
Egg wash (1 egg yolk beaten with 1 tablespoon cold water)

In a Dutch oven, brown the chicken on all sides in the oil for about 15 minutes. Drain off the oil and add the water, *bouquet garni*, whole onions, carrots, and celery stalks to the chicken. Season and simmer until the chicken is done, about 1 hour.

Meanwhile, fry the bacon pieces, drain on paper towels, and reserve. Fry the sausage slices in the bacon drippings and also drain and reserve. Prepare either of the pie crusts and set aside until the pie is ready to put together.

To assemble, lift the chicken gently into an oval or rectangular casserole—the chicken should be higher than the sides of the dish. Surround it with the leeks, sausage, bacon, and chopped parsley. Add the vermouth and one cup of the chicken stock, strained. Correct the seasoning.

Roll out the pie crust on a floured surface and cover the chicken, letting the pie crust fall over it. Secure the edge of the crust under the rim of the casserole and decorate the top with cutout pieces of leftover dough, securing them with dabs of egg wash. Slash the pie crust in several places for steam to escape and bake the chicken in a preheated 375-degree oven until the pie crust is brown, about 30 minutes. Ten minutes before the crust is done, brush the top with egg wash and continue baking.

CHICKEN PIE CRUST

1/2 pound all-purpose flour, weighed, not measured
1/2 stick (4 tablespoons) butter, at room temperature
2 ounces cream cheese, at room temperature

1 large egg, beaten
1 teaspoon salt
Iced water, enough to make a stiff dough

Combine all the ingredients, and work well.

ALTERNATE CRUST

Defrost 1-1/2 packets of frozen patty shells. When they are pliable, combine them and form a ball of dough.

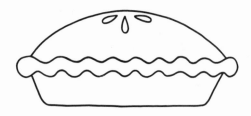

SHARON'S CHICKEN IN SOUR CREAM

Serves 4

3 pounds chicken pieces	1 cup sliced fresh mushrooms
Salt and pepper	3 tablespoons chopped parsley
1 stick (1/4 pound) butter	3 whole scallions, chopped
2 tablespoons all-purpose flour	1/4 cup water
1 pint sour cream	1 teaspoon paprika, or to taste

Wash and dry the chicken pieces, then salt and pepper them and brown them in the butter in a skillet, taking care not to burn the butter. Remove the chicken to a 2-quart casserole. Reheat the butter and blend in the flour; cook, stirring, for about 3 minutes. Cool thoroughly, then gradually add the sour cream, stirring with a wire whisk, and simmer over low heat for a few minutes. Do not boil it or the sour cream will curdle. Pour the sauce over the chicken and add all the other ingredients except the paprika. Cover and bake at 325 degrees for 1 to 1-1/2 hours or until tender.

Season the sauce with salt and paprika when the chicken is done.

MARINATED CHICKEN WITH RAISINS

Chicken baked in a wine marinade, and laced with brandy-soaked raisins.

Serves 4 to 6

2 cups dry wine, white or red
3 to 4 carrots, scraped and
   halved
2 stalks celery, halved
2 large red onions, peeled and
   sliced
1 bay leaf
4 sprigs parsley
2 cloves garlic, peeled and
   halved

12 peppercorns
4 pounds chicken pieces
Cooking oil
Salt
2 tablespoons cornstarch
2 to 3 tablespoons water
1/3 cup brandy
2/3 cup raisins

Combine the wine, carrots, celery, onion, bay leaf, parsley, garlic, and peppercorns and marinate the chicken in this mixture overnight.

Drain the chicken and reserve the marinade. Dry the pieces as well as possible and brown them, a few at a time, in the oil. Season and transfer them to a casserole. Combine the cornstarch with about 2 to 3 tablespoons water and stir it into the marinade. Add this mixture to the casserole.

Heat, but do not boil, the brandy and raisins until the raisins are plump—about 5 or 10 minutes. Add to the casserole and bake, covered, at 400 degrees until the chicken is done, about 45 minutes to 1 hour.

COQ AU VIN, LE PROVENÇAL

Serves 4 to 6

2 fryers, cut into serving pieces
Salt, pepper, and thyme
Butter
2/3 cup cubed bacon
2/3 cup sliced fresh mushrooms
10 pearl onions
About 2 tablespoons Cognac
2 cloves garlic, peeled and
  crushed

1 bay leaf
1 bottle Burgundy
Beurre manié: 2 tablespoons
  softened butter combined
  with 1-1/2 tablespoons
  all-purpose flour
Croûtons, fried in butter

Season the chicken with salt, pepper, and thyme and sauté the pieces in butter until golden brown. In another pan sauté the bacon about a minute, then add the mushrooms and onions and sauté until golden brown. Transfer this mixture to a casserole, then place the chicken pieces on top.

Deglaze the sauté pans with the Cognac, and put the contents in the larger pan. Add the garlic, bay leaf, and wine and bring this mixture to a rolling boil. Boil until the liquid is reduced by half. Add it to the chicken and cook, covered, in a 400-degree oven for about 10 minutes per pound, or until the chicken is tender.

Put the casserole on top of the stove. Add the *beurre manié*, bit by bit, while stirring vigorously. Simmer, stirring, long enough for the sauce to thicken. Decorate with croûtons.

CHICKEN WITH CRANBERRIES

A cranberry compote is poured over browned chicken, and slices of orange peel give the dish an added fruit flavor.

Serves 4

3 pounds chicken pieces
2 cloves garlic, peeled and cut
Salt and lemon pepper
1/4 cup cooking oil
1 large red onion, peeled and
    sliced

1/4 cup Bourbon
1-1/2 cups raw cranberries
1/4 cup brown sugar
1/2 cup water
1 large orange, washed but not
    peeled, and sliced

Rub the chicken with the garlic and season with the salt and lemon pepper. Heat the oil in a skillet and brown the chicken, a few pieces at a time. Transfer the browned pieces to a casserole. Sauté the onion slices in the same skillet until golden brown, then transfer with a slotted spoon to the casserole and discard all the fat from the skillet. Add the Bourbon and stir and scrape until all particles are loose and the pan is deglazed. Pour this liquid over the chicken.

In a saucepan combine and simmer the cranberries, sugar, and water until the berries disintegrate a little—about 5 to 10 minutes. Pour the compote over the chicken. Top with sliced oranges. Cover the casserole and bake in a preheated oven at 400 degrees for 1 hour, or until the chicken is very tender.

CHICKEN GUMBO

The famous "long-simmered" Southern dish—with rice, tomatoes, okra. A complete meal.

Serves 8

4 pounds chicken pieces
All-purpose flour
1/4 cup cooking oil
2 tablespoons butter
3 medium-sized onions, peeled
   and sliced
1 ham bone or ham hock

4 large tomatoes, peeled,
   seeded, and chopped
4 cups fresh okra, sliced in rings
3/4 cup finely chopped celery
   leaves
Salt and cayenne pepper
8 to 10 cups cold water

Roll the chicken pieces in flour and shake off any excess. Heat the oil and butter in a large skillet and brown the chicken pieces evenly to a golden brown, then transfer them to a soup kettle.

Sauté the onions in the fat in the skillet until golden brown. Remove with a slotted spoon and add to the kettle. Add all the remaining ingredients, cover, and simmer over low heat until the meat of the chicken drops from the bones—about 2-1/2 to 3 hours. Remove as many bones as possible and serve the gumbo over rice.

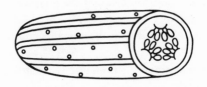

CHICKEN CASSEROLE WITH
40 CLOVES OF GARLIC

A layered casserole dish with spectacular garlic to spread on
toast. If you want to do this with chicken breasts, see page 40.

Serves 6

2 fryers, cut into serving pieces
Cooking oil
Salt and pepper
2 medium eggplants, cut into
    strips as for large-sized
    French fries
2 large red onions, peeled and
    sliced
4 green peppers, seeded and
    cut in strips

40 or so cloves garlic, peeled
    but uncut. (It is important
    that the cloves not be cut.
    This way the garlic is more
    like a vegetable and does not
    have the powerful taste or
    smell associated with its raw
    form.)
2 cups dry vermouth
1/4 cup brandy

Brown the chicken pieces on all sides in oil, using a large skillet and cooking just a few pieces at a time. Season with salt and pepper while cooking. When the chicken is browned, reserve.

Clean the skillet and brown the eggplant slices in a small amount of oil and reserve in a large bowl. Then sauté first the onions and then the pepper in oil and add to the eggplant. Season and mix well. Place the chicken, vegetables, and raw garlic in alternate layers in a large casserole. Season each layer lightly. Combine the vermouth and brandy and pour over the chicken. Cover tightly.

Bake at 400 degrees in a preheated oven for about 1-1/2 hours. And don't lift the cover until the casserole is on the table. Serve each person with enough of the soft, aromatic garlic to spread on toast.

CHICKEN CASSEROLE WITH TOMATO PURÉE AND WINE

Here the chicken pieces are first roasted and then casseroled with a white wine-tomato sauce.

Serves 6

4 pounds chicken pieces	1 large onion, peeled and cut in
Salt	wedges
1/2 cup chicken or beef stock or	3 cloves garlic, peeled
consommé	1 cup dry white wine
2 tablespoons Dijon-style	2/3 cup tomato purée
mustard	

Season the chicken pieces on both sides with salt. Bake in an oiled baking pan, skin side up, at 375 degrees until the chicken is golden brown and almost done—about 45 to 50 minutes.

Meanwhile, in an electric blender, combine the stock, mustard, onion, and garlic; blend until quite smooth. Combine this mixture with the wine and tomato purée.

Transfer the chicken pieces to a casserole, pour the sauce over the chicken, and cover the casserole. (This far the casserole can be done some hours or even a day ahead of time.)

Bake at 375 degrees for 45 minutes or more if the casserole was chilled before baking, or until the chicken is done.

BONED, AND MOSTLY BREASTS

EGG AND CHICKEN CASSEROLE

Cubed chicken, eggs in the shell, and chickpeas simmer in a cumin- and turmeric-flavored sauce. An Indian dish that goes beautifully with rice.

Serves 8

8 eggs
1/4 cup cooking oil
3 large onions, peeled and
   sliced thin
2 cloves garlic, peeled and
   crushed
3 pounds boned chicken meat,
   in large cubes
2 chicken bouillon cubes
1 cup boiling water
1-1/2 cups chickpeas, soaked
   overnight in cold water

3 potatoes, peeled and diced
3 carrots, scraped and diced
1 cup dried currants
1 teaspoon ground turmeric
1 tablespoon ground cumin
1 bay leaf
1/2 teaspoon freshly ground
   pepper, or more to taste
Salt to taste

Scrub the eggs in cold water until very clean and reserve. Heat the oil in a large skillet. Add the onions and sauté for about 10 minutes, or until golden brown, stirring often. Add the garlic and some of the chicken cubes and sauté in batches, no more than 3 minutes, until all the chicken cubes are lightly browned. Transfer with a slotted spoon to a casserole each time a batch is brown. Pour out most of the oil.

Dissolve the bouillon cubes in the boiling water and deglaze the skillet, scraping and stirring. Add this liquid to the casserole.

Drain the chickpeas and add them to the casserole. Add the remaining ingredients, and carefully nestle in the eggs. Add water to cover. Cover the casserole tightly, first with foil and then the lid. Bake at 300 degrees for at least 3 hours. Serve with rice.

CHICKEN AND TONGUE CASSEROLE

A simple and unusual recipe.

Serves 4

8 chicken breast halves, boned, with the skin on
All-purpose flour
8 slices cooked tongue (or country ham)

1 cup chicken stock or broth
1 cup yogurt
1/2 cup dry sherry
Pepper (no salt if the tongue is salty)

Dredge the chicken in flour and shake off the excess. Arrange the chicken and tongue in alternate layers in a casserole, ending with the chicken, skin side up to protect the delicate meat. Combine the remaining ingredients and pour over the chicken. Bake, covered, for 40 minutes at 375 degrees. Uncover and bake until the chicken is done and the sauce thickens and coats the meat—about 20 more minutes.

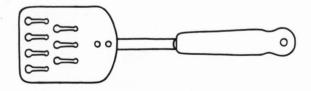

CHICKEN BREASTS WITH
40 CLOVES OF GARLIC

Serves 6

12 small chicken breast halves
Cooking oil
Salt and freshly ground black
    pepper
2 pounds eggplant, zucchini or
    other squash, or a mixture of
    all

2 large red onions, sliced
2 cups dry white wine
1/4 cup brandy
40 cloves garlic, peeled but
    uncut

Brown the chicken breasts, a few at a time, in some oil, no more than 2 minutes on each side; season while cooking. Reserve them.

Slice the eggplant or squash into rounds or cut into strips and sauté them in the same pan, adding a little more oil if necessary. Again season while cooking and reserve. Sauté the onion rings until golden brown and reserve. Combine the wine and brandy and deglaze the pan with this mixture.

To assemble, place the vegetables and chicken pieces in layers in a casserole, putting some of the raw garlic between each layer. Add the wine mixture. Cover well and bake, *without* lifting the lid, for 1 hour and 40 minutes at 400 degrees. Serve each person with some of the stewed garlic to be spread on thin rye toast.

CHICKEN BREASTS WITH GRAPES

In this delicate dish the chicken breasts are combined with a little wine and some seedless grapes.

Serves 4

8 chicken breast halves, boned (boned thighs may also be used)	Salt and pepper
	1/4 cup chopped scallion bulbs
	1 large clove garlic, minced
All-purpose flour	1 cup dry white wine
1/2 stick (4 tablespoons) butter	1/2 cup water
1 teaspoon ground mace	1 cup seedless grapes

Dust the chicken breasts with flour; sauté them in butter to brown, no more than 2 minutes on each side (longer for boned dark meat). Season them with the mace and salt and pepper while cooking. Reserve them while you sauté the onions and garlic briefly; then place the breasts in a casserole, scattering the aromatics and butter in and around.

Combine the wine and water and deglaze the skillet, scraping and stirring. Pour the liquid over the chicken and add the grapes. Cover and bake in a preheated oven at 400 degrees for 40 minutes or until the chicken is done.

In the Skillet

FRIED, SAUTÉED, BROWNED AND SIMMERED

*In this chapter first come a few fried or sautéed chickens,
uncovered, then lots of browned and simmered in the frying pan,
and finally a number of elegant boned chicken breast sautés.*

*The emphasis is international—here are recipes such as Pollo
Alla Aglio e Olio, Masala Chicken, Arroz con Pollo, Chicken
Breasts au Poivre Vert, Chicken Kiev, Spicy Chinese Chicken . . .*

TO FRY A CHICKEN

Remember that chicken pieces aren't flat. For oil to reach every
part of a chicken piece, it must come halfway up the chicken or
there will be a raw white band around the center of each piece
after both sides are cooked. This might mean as much as 2-1/2
inches of oil or more for deep frying. For deep frying, all of the
chicken pieces are submerged in boiling oil—usually a few at a
time in a frying basket. No turning of the chicken pieces will be
necessary, only an occasional shaking of the basket. Oil, not
butter, should be used. Butter has a lower boiling point than oil, so
it will burn before oil does. If a thermometer is used, the oil
should be kept between 360 and 380 degrees. Never add more
than 1 piece of chicken to the oil at one time, or the temperature of
the oil will drop. If the chicken is fried in a skillet, the pieces
shouldn't touch, since if the pan is too crowded steaming will take
place rather than frying.

TO SAUTÉ A CHICKEN

There are two main kinds of sautéing; a white sauté and a brown sauté.

The white sauté is for chicken cooked with a light-colored sauce—sometimes cream or white wine is added, sometimes both.

Brown sautéing gives color and flavor to the dish that is being cooked. Often the pan is deglazed (particles are scraped off the bottom with liquid) and this is incorporated in the sauce. At times red wine is added to further color and flavor this sauce.

For all sautéing butter or oil can be used, since the source of heat is lower than for frying. I prefer a combination of butter and oil—oil because it doesn't burn as easily as butter, and butter to flavor the oil. If butter alone is used, it should be clarified first, since the milky residue in butter burns more easily than the fatty liquid. This is more important for a white sauté.

To clarify butter: melt the butter over low heat. Pour off the clear yellow fat and discard the residue, the milky part. The butter is now clarified.

CHICKEN PIECES

AUSTRIAN FRIED CHICKEN *(BACKHENDEL)*

This is the spring chicken fried in bread crumbs I loved as a child in Vienna.

Serves 4 to 6

2 broilers, in small serving pieces, at room temperature
Salt and pepper
All-purpose flour
3 eggs
Bread crumbs

Rendered lard or vegetable shortening (not oil)
1 stick (1/4 pound) plus 1 tablespoon butter
2 cloves garlic, peeled and halved

Pat the chicken dry. Mix salt and pepper into the flour—about 1 teaspoon of salt to 2 cups flour. Beat the eggs lightly. Dip the chicken pieces in the seasoned flour, patting as much flour onto each piece as it will hold. Next dip the floured pieces into the beaten egg. Turn each piece in the egg, then coat with as many of the bread crumbs as possible. Spread the coated chicken on waxed paper in 1 layer and let the coating dry at room temperature for at least 1 hour.

Heat the lard or shortening, the 1 tablespoon butter, and the garlic in a large skillet. The fat should be 1 to 2 inches deep. Fry the larger pieces first, over moderate heat, until golden brown— about 10 minutes on each side. Turn only once. The chicken pieces should not touch each other during cooking.

Remove with a spatula or slotted spoon and place in a baking pan. Heat the oven to 350 degrees, then, keeping the oven door ajar, place the fried pieces in the oven to keep warm while cooking the remaining ones. Melt the stick of butter and pour a little on each piece of cooked chicken.

POLLO ALLA AGLIO E OLIO

This is "Chicken with Oil and Garlic."

Serves 4

1 roasting chicken, 3 pounds,
   cut into very small pieces
3 tablespoons olive oil
3 large cloves garlic, peeled and
   crushed

1/2 cup dry white wine
1/2 teaspoon oregano
Salt and pepper
A handful of chopped parsley

Brown the chicken pieces over moderate heat in the olive oil, turning them. After about 5 minutes add the crushed garlic and continue to cook, turning, for 5 to 7 minutes more. Add the wine, oregano, and salt and pepper and cook over low heat until the chicken is done, about 30 minutes. Just before serving, sprinkle in the chopped parsley and toss the chicken briefly.

CHICKEN CACCIATORE, LA SCALA, NEW YORK

Another Italian sauté, this one simmers in a wine, mushroom, and tomato sauce.

Serves 3

1 fryer, cut into very small
    pieces
All-purpose flour
2 tablespoons butter
Olive oil
1 small onion, chopped
1 tomato, peeled and chopped

1/2 cup sliced fresh mushrooms
1 tablespoon prosciutto ham,
    chopped
1-1/2 cups chicken broth
1 cup dry white wine
Salt, pepper, and oregano to
    taste

Dust the chicken in flour and brown the pieces in the butter and about 1 tablespoon olive oil. Add the onion and sauté until golden brown. Drain off the oil, add the rest of the ingredients, and simmer until the chicken is done and the sauce begins to thicken. Remove the chicken to a serving platter and keep warm while you stir the sauce over high heat to let it thicken. Taste for seasoning and pour over the chicken.

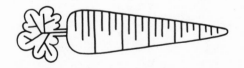

DARK MEAT WITH GREEN PEPPERCORNS

Serves 4

8 to 12 chicken thighs	1 cup chicken stock
4 tablespoons cooking oil	1 cup cream
1/2 to 1 stick (4 to 8 tablespoons) butter	3 tablespoons green peppercorns
1/4 cup brandy	Salt to taste

With a sharp knife, cut along the bone on the meat side of each thigh and scrape the flesh away from the bone. Place the boned chicken pieces between waxed paper and pound to flatten them. Salt them lightly.

Heat 2 tablespoons of oil and 3 or 4 of butter in a large skillet. Brown some of the chicken on both sides and cook for about 15 minutes, or until the chicken is done. Repeat until all the chicken is cooked, adding oil and butter as needed. Transfer the chicken to a serving platter and keep hot.

Pour off excess fat from the skillet, add the brandy, and ignite, shaking the pan until the flames are extinguished. Add the stock and deglaze the pan, scraping and stirring. Add the cream and boil the sauce rapidly to reduce the sauce by almost half. Add the peppercorns, correct the seasoning, and pour over the chicken to serve.

CHICKEN IN SAUCE MARCHAND DE VIN

Chicken in a rich, winy sauce that includes bits of ham or tongue.

Serves 6

1/2 cup cooking oil
5 pounds chicken pieces
1 stick (1/4 pound) butter
1 large onion, minced
1/2 cup fresh mushroom stems, minced
4 to 6 shallots, minced
2 cloves garlic, minced
1 cup ham or tongue, cooked and diced

1/4 cup all-purpose flour
Salt and cayenne pepper to taste
1-1/2 cups consommé or brown stock
1-1/2 cups dry red wine

Heat the oil in a skillet and brown the chicken pieces on all sides in batches. Put the chicken aside. Pour out the oil in the pan, heat the butter, and sauté the onion to a golden brown, stirring often. Add the mushroom stems, shallots, garlic, and ham or tongue and continue to cook and stir for 5 to 10 minutes more. Add the flour and seasonings and sauté, stirring, to a rich brown. Add the consommé or stock and the red wine; stir to blend in all the flavors, then add the chicken and allow to simmer for 40 minutes, or until the chicken is done. Correct seasoning and serve.

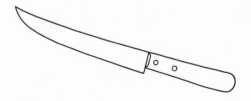

RUMANIAN CHICKEN

Serves 4

6 slices bacon, or blanched salt
    pork
4-pound chicken, cut into small
    serving pieces
1 clove garlic, minced
2 leeks, cleaned and sliced
    (bulbs only)
2 kohlrabi, sliced
1 cup green peas
1 cup cooked white (navy)
    beans

2 tablespoons granulated sugar
1 tablespoon vinegar
2 teaspoons ground cumin seed
2 teaspoons ground caraway
    seed
2 cups chicken stock
3 tablespoons butter
3 tablespoons all-purpose flour
Salt and pepper to taste

Render the bacon or salt pork in a skillet, then remove with a
slotted spoon and reserve to use another time. Brown the chicken
pieces in the rendered fat, a few at a time. Set the chicken aside.

In the same skillet sauté the garlic, leeks, and kohlrabi for about
5 to 7 minutes, stirring occasionally. Add the peas and cooked
beans and sauté for 2 to 3 minutes. Pour out as much accumulated
fat as possible, then sprinkle the sugar over the vegetables and
stir. When the sugar has caramelized, sprinkle the vinegar over
the vegetables and stir. Add the cumin and caraway seed. Return
the chicken to the pan or skillet and add the chicken stock.

Combine the butter and flour to make a *beurre manié* and add as
much of it to the sauce, a bit at a time, as is needed to give it the
desired consistency. Season and simmer the chicken in the sauce
until the chicken is done, about 30 to 40 minutes.

CHICKEN PAPRIKA

A spicy chicken with lots of onions.

Serves 6

4 pounds onions, chopped
1/4 cup cooking oil
1 tablespoon butter
4 pounds chicken pieces
3 cloves garlic, minced
3 or 4 tablespoons sweet
   Hungarian paprika

2 tablespoons Dijon-style
   mustard
3 teaspoons salt, or to taste
1 cup water or chicken stock,
   more if needed

Sauté the onions in the oil and butter until mushy and golden brown, about 15 to 20 minutes, stirring often. Add the chicken pieces and garlic and sauté, stirring, until the chicken too has taken on color. Add the paprika, mustard, salt, and some of the water or stock. Cover and simmer until the chicken is done, about 40 minutes. Stir at times, adding more liquid as necessary.

VARIATION

Just before serving, beat 3 egg yolks into 6 tablespoons sour cream and add this mixture to the chicken. Cook only long enough to heat through; the sauce should thicken slightly. Stir constantly and avoid bringing the sauce to a boil or it will curdle.

CHICKEN WITH PAPRIKA RICE

A good big dish—with sausage, peppers, tomatoes, scallions.

Serves 4

1 fryer, whole or in serving
   pieces
Cooking oil
1 pound, or more, Polish
   sausage, in 1-inch pieces
6 to 8 whole scallions, chopped
2 green peppers, seeded and
   chopped
2 cloves garlic, minced
   (optional)

1 large tomato, peeled and
   chopped
1 tablespoon sweet Hungarian
   paprika, or more to taste
1 tablespoon salt
2 cups chicken stock
1 cup dry white wine
1-1/2 cups raw long-grain rice
1/2 cup chopped parsley

If you are cooking the chicken whole, select a Dutch oven with a well-fitting lid. If you are cooking the chicken in pieces, a large, deep skillet with a well-fitting lid will do. Brown the chicken or chicken pieces, uncovered, in as little oil as possible. Set aside the chicken and brown the sausage in the same pan. Reserve. Still in the same pan, sauté the scallions and peppers until soft, about 10 minutes. Add the garlic, tomato, paprika, and salt; stir. Add the liquids and deglaze the pan. Return the chicken and simmer, covered, until the chicken is done—about 25 minutes for pieces and about 45 minutes for a whole chicken. Return the sausage to the pan and add the rice. Cook, covered, over minimum heat for 15 to 20 minutes, or until the rice has the desired consistency. Add the parsley and stir with a fork.

MASALA CHICKEN

The spices, made into a paste, add up to curry—this is the way the dish is created in India.

Serves 2 to 3

Cooking oil
1 fryer, about 3 pounds, cut
  into serving pieces
3 medium-sized onions, peeled
  and sliced
3 tomatoes, peeled and cut up
2 dried red chili peppers,
  crushed
1/2 teaspoon freshly ground
  pepper
1 large clove garlic, peeled and
  crushed
1 teaspoon ground cinnamon
1 teaspoon ground ginger
1 teaspoon turmeric
1 teaspoon ground cumin seed
1 teaspoon paprika
1 teaspoon salt
Garnish: slices of red onion and
  lemon

Heat some cooking oil in a very large skillet and brown the chicken pieces on both sides. Reserve. Discard excess oil, scrape the pan, and brown the onions lightly. Add the tomatoes. Combine the remaining ingredients with 1 tablespoon of cooking oil to form a paste, add 1 cup of water to it, and stir. Return the chicken pieces to the skillet and pour the spicy paste over the chicken. Cook covered, over medium heat for 30 to 35 minutes, stirring at times. Uncover and cook over high heat, stirring often, until the chicken is done and the paste is all but absorbed, about 7 to 10 minutes. Serve with slices of red onion and lemon.

Rice makes a good side dish.

CHICKEN CURRY

Here is a simple curry-sauce chicken with raisins.

Serves 6

1/2 cup cooking oil	2 to 3 tablespoons Madras curry
2 chickens, 3 pounds each, cut	powder, or more to taste
into small serving pieces	1-1/2 cups raisins
2 large red onions, sliced thin	About 1 cup water
3 tablespoons all-purpose flour	Salt

Heat the oil in a heavy skillet and brown the chicken pieces on all sides. Remove with a slotted spoon and reserve. Add the onions to the oil and sauté to a golden brown, about 10 minutes. Discard excess fat if any, return the chicken to the pan, and sprinkle the flour and curry powder over the chicken and onions. Stir and cook for a few minutes. Then add the raisins and about 1 cup of water and stir well to incorporate all particles from the bottom and the sides. Cover and simmer over low heat until the chicken is done, about 50 minutes. Add more water as necessary. Season with salt.

Serve with boiled rice, chutney, raw onion rings, chopped peanuts, etc. The spiciness of this dish would be beautifully offset by a side dish of very cold fruit, such as melon balls.

CHICKEN WITH GINGER CHUTNEY

Serves 2 to 3

1/4 cup cooking oil	2 tablespoons cornstarch
2 tablespoons butter	1/4 cup dry sherry
1 large fryer, cut into small pieces	1-1/2 cups chicken stock
	1 teaspoon curry powder
1 medium-sized onion, peeled and sliced thin	1 teaspoon ground cumin seed
	Salt and freshly ground pepper
1 clove garlic, peeled and crushed	1/2 cup sour cream

Combine the oil and butter and brown the chicken pieces all over. Remove with a slotted spoon and reserve. Sauté the onion and garlic in the same skillet until both are limp and golden brown. Discard all but 2 to 3 tablespoons of fat and return the chicken to the skillet. Combine the cornstarch and sherry and add to the skillet, stirring. Then add the chicken stock slowly, still stirring. Add the curry powder, cumin, salt, and pepper. Cover the skillet and simmer until the chicken tests done, about 45 minutes. Remove the chicken, skim off any excess fat from the sauce, stir in the sour cream, and pour the sauce over the chicken. Serve at once with ginger chutney (below) and rice.

NOTE: If the chicken is done ahead of time, do not add the sour cream until just before serving.

GINGER CHUTNEY
To be used in small quantities.

1/2 cup vinegar	2 large fresh ginger roots, peeled
1/2 cup raisins	
1/2 cup brown sugar	

Bring the vinegar to a boil and add the raisins. Turn off the heat and let the raisins plump while you chop the ginger fine. Add the brown sugar and ginger to the saucepan and simmer this mixture until the liquid thickens, about 3 to 5 minutes. Cool to room temperature to serve.

NOTE: Any leftover chutney must be refrigerated. It does not keep long.

ARROZ CON POLLO

The famous Spanish chicken with saffron-flavored rice.

Serves 6 to 8

1 slice ham or 6 slices bacon, diced
1/2 cup cooking oil
2 large fryers, cut into small serving pieces
2 onions, approximately 1 pound, chopped
4 cloves garlic, or to taste, minced
3 to 4 green peppers and/or red pimientos, chopped
2 cups water, more if necessary
A good pinch saffron
1 tablespoon salt
Pepper to taste
2 cups raw long-grain rice
1 package frozen corn and/or peas, defrosted

Sauté the ham or bacon until crisp, drain on paper towels, and reserve. Pour out most of the fat if you use bacon. Add and heat the oil; brown the chicken pieces, a few at a time, on all sides. Reserve. Add the onions, garlic, and peppers and sauté for 5 minutes. Return the chicken pieces and bacon to the pan. Add the water, saffron, salt, and pepper.

Cover and simmer over low heat until the chicken is done, about 30 to 40 minutes. The liquid in the pan should measure 3 cups or a little more; add water if necessary. Bring the liquid to a rolling boil and add the rice. Stir once or twice, cover the pan, reduce the heat to a minimum, and cook the dish 15 to 20 minutes more. Add the frozen vegetables, stir with a fork to fluff the rice, and cook, covered, only long enough for the vegetables to heat through.

CHICKEN WITH BOUQUET GARNI

Chicken browned and then simmered in a wine and tomato sauce, lightly thickened with cream at the end.

Serves 4 to 6

6 slices bacon, cut into 1-inch
   pieces
5 pounds chicken pieces
3 tablespoons instant-cooking
   flour
1 cup chicken stock
2 to 3 cups dry white wine

1 *bouquet garni*: about 2 sprigs
   parsley, 1/2 bay leaf, 1 sprig
   or 1/8 teaspoon thyme tied in
   cheesecloth
2 cloves garlic, peeled and
   crushed (optional)
8-ounce can peeled tomatoes
Salt and pepper
1/4 cup heavy cream

Render the bacon (discard or eat it) and brown the chicken pieces in the drippings, in batches if necessary. Pour out most of the fat. Combine the flour and stock and add to the chicken, stirring. Add all the other ingredients but the cream. Cover and simmer until the chicken is tender, about 1 hour.

Transfer the chicken to a hot platter and keep hot. Discard the *bouquet garni*, skim off excess fat, add the cream, and stir over high heat until the sauce thickens a little. Season to taste and pour the sauce over the chicken to serve.

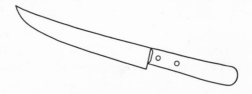

FRICASSEE OF CHICKEN WITH
PEAS AND MUSHROOMS

A delicate wine sauce is thickened with egg yolks and cream, and poured over chicken, peas, and mushrooms.

Serves 2 or 3

3-pound chicken, cut into small
   pieces
Salt and white pepper to taste
2 tablespoons cooking oil
3 tablespoons butter
1 clove garlic, peeled and
   crushed
4 shallots, minced
2 tablespoons all-purpose flour
1 cup dry white wine

1 cup chicken stock or broth
1 *bouquet garni*: about 2 sprigs
   parsley, 1/2 bay leaf, 1 sprig
   or 1/8 teaspoon thyme tied in
   cheesecloth
1 cup small mushrooms,
   destemmed
1 cup fresh green peas
2 egg yolks
1/4 cup heavy cream

Season the chicken with salt and pepper. Combine and heat the oil and butter in a heavy saucepan. Gently sauté the chicken pieces, if necessary a few at a time, on all sides; do not let butter and oil burn. Assemble the pieces in the pan and add the garlic, shallots, and flour, stirring them into the oil. Add the wine slowly while stirring. Add the stock, *bouquet garni*, and mushrooms. Cover with a tight-fitting lid and simmer over very low heat for approximately 25 minutes. Add the peas, cover again, and simmer until the chicken and the peas are tender—approximately 10 minutes more.

Turn off the heat and remove and discard the *bouquet garni*. Transfer the chicken pieces to a hot platter and keep hot. Skim any excess fat off the sauce. Beat the egg yolks well with the cream. Slowly pour about 1 cup of the sauce into the egg mixture while beating, and then add this egg mixture to the sauce. Reheat without boiling, season to taste, and pour the sauce over the chicken.

CHICKEN PORKELT

This is a Hungarian chicken stew. Since Hungarian cuisine is almost always based on some kind of pork fat, it's important not to substitute the bacon or salt pork.

Serves 6

1 cup slab bacon or salt pork, diced

2 chickens, about 2-1/2 to 3 pounds each, cut up, with necks, gizzards, and liver included

2 very large red onions, chopped

2 green or red bell peppers, seeded and chopped

1 or 2 cloves garlic, minced

2 tablespoons or more sweet Hungarian paprika

6-ounce can tomato purée

2 cups chicken stock

1 large dill pickle, sliced thin

Salt

1 cup sour cream

Blanch the bacon or salt pork in boiling water for 5 minutes. Dry as well as possible on paper towels and sauté in a skillet to a golden brown. Remove with a slotted spoon, drain on paper towels, and reserve.

Brown the chicken, including the neck, gizzards, and liver, in the rendered fat, a few pieces at a time; drain and reserve. Discard almost all the fat. Sauté the onions, peppers, and garlic in the remaining drippings for about 10 minutes.

Return the chicken and bacon or salt pork to the pan. Add the paprika. tomato purée, stock, and sliced pickle. Season with salt and simmer, covered, until the chicken is done, about 1 hour, or less. Stir in the sour cream and heat but do not boil. Serve with noodles or *Nockerln*, a kind of dumpling.

CHICKEN BREASTS

BREADED CHICKEN BREASTS

A very simple sautéed chicken breast, one of the best ways to do it.

Per person

1 egg
1 tablespoon water
Salt and pepper
2 chicken breast halves, boned, skinned, and pounded paper thin

All-purpose flour
Bread crumbs
2 tablespoons cooking oil
1 tablespoon butter
Ham or fried bacon

Beat the egg with the tablespoon of water. Add salt and pepper and beat again. Dip each piece of chicken first in flour, then in the egg, and last into bread crumbs—patting on as many bread crumbs as each piece will hold. Leave to dry at room temperature for 1 hour, or several hours in the refrigerator.

Combine the oil and butter in the skillet and sauté each piece over medium heat until golden on both sides—about 3 minutes per side. Do not overcook or the chicken will dry out. Serve each piece on a slice of ham, or topped with several slices of bacon.

CHICKEN BREASTS AU POIVRE VERT

A garlic and green peppercorn paste makes this simple sautéed dish very tasty and unusual.

Per person

1 small clove garlic, peeled	1 tablespoon clarified butter
2 teaspoons green peppercorns	(see page 46)
2 chicken breast halves, boned	1/4 cup dry vermouth

Crush the garlic and peppercorns in a mortar. Rub this mixture into both sides of the chicken breasts. Leave at room temperature for 1 hour.

Heat the clarified butter in a skillet. Sauté the chicken breasts until done, about 8 minutes, turning them 2 or 3 times during cooking. Add the vermouth and deglaze the pan. Serve hot.

NOTE: Green peppercorns are available pickled in brine or in vinegar. I prefer those kept in brine. Green peppercorns are not as hot as dried peppercorns.

CHICKEN FLORENTINE

That elegant Italian creation—cheese-covered chicken breasts on a bed of spinach.

Serves 4

8 chicken breast halves, boned and skinned
Salt
All-purpose flour
2 eggs, beaten
1/3 cup cooking oil

2 pounds spinach, cooked, well drained, and chopped
2 tablespoons butter
1/4 cup grated Parmesan
8 slices mozzarella

Preheat the oven to 350 degrees.

Combine salt and flour in a plastic bag; shake the chicken breasts in this mixture to coat them. Dip them in beaten eggs, and then sauté in the oil over low heat until cooked, turning once. The chicken should take about 8 to 10 minutes in all.

On an ovenproof serving platter arrange the hot spinach mixed with the butter and place the chicken breasts on the bed of spinach. Sprinkle each piece with some Parmesan and top with mozzarella. Place in the preheated oven long enough for the cheese to melt, about 5 to 10 minutes.

CHICKEN BIRDS CORDON BLEU

Chicken breasts wrapped around Gruyère and prosciutto and fried.

Serves 4

8 chicken breast halves, boned
  and skinned
4 large slices prosciutto or
  Westphalian ham
4 large slices Gruyère
All-purpose flour
2 eggs beaten with 1/4 cup milk

1 cup bread crumbs mixed with
  1-1/2 teaspoons salt and 1-1/2
  teaspoons dry mustard
2/3 cup cooking oil
2 tablespoons butter
1 or 2 cloves garlic, peeled and
  halved

Pound each of the 8 pieces of chicken breast between waxed paper until very thin but not broken. Cut thin slices of prosciutto or Westphalian ham to about half the size of the pounded chicken pieces. Place 1 piece of meat in the center of each piece of chicken. Roll a half slice of cheese like a fat cigarette and place on the ham. Roll up each chicken breast around the filling, taking care to tuck in the sides to prevent leakage. If necessary secure with toothpicks.

Dip each "bird" first in flour, then the egg mixture. Shake off excess egg and roll each piece in the seasoned bread crumbs. Allow to dry at room temperature on waxed paper for 1 hour, or in the refrigerator for several hours.

Heat the oil, butter, and garlic in a large skillet. Gently fry the chicken birds to a golden brown, turning frequently. Do not cook them longer than 8 to 10 minutes. Drain them on paper towels.

NOTE: Do not let the birds touch one another in the skillet; if necessary cook in batches or in 2 skillets.

CHICKEN KIEV

The spectacular chicken around herb butter.

Serves 4

3 tablespoons very finely
  minced shallots
1/4 cup dry vermouth
2 sticks (1/2 pound) butter,
  more if necessary, at room
  temperature
1/4 teaspoon dry mustard
8 chicken breast halves, boned,
  with the first joint of the
  wing, including the bone,
  attached

2 to 3 eggs
2 tablespoons cream or milk,
  more if necessary
All-purpose flour
Bread crumbs
Salt and pepper
1 cup cooking oil, more if
  necessary

Combine the shallots and vermouth and simmer over very low heat until the vermouth has evaporated and the shallots are limp. Cool completely. Meanwhile, bring 1 stick of the butter to room temperature. With a fork combine the shallots, butter, and mustard. Reshape to resemble a stick of butter and refrigerate for several hours, or freeze for 1 hour. When the butter mixture is cold, cut it in half. Quarter each half lengthwise, to form 8 sticks. Freeze each stick separately.

Pound each chicken breast half between waxed paper until thin and spread out. Place 1 stick of the frozen butter on each piece of chicken. Fold the pointed end of the chicken over the butter and roll the rest of the chicken around it to enclose it completely. The chicken breast half should now resemble a triangle in shape, with the first joint of the chicken wing sticking out at a right angle.

Combine 2 eggs and the milk or cream, beating lightly. You may need more eggs and milk.

Dip the rolled chicken first in flour, then in the egg mixture, and coat well with bread crumbs. Season and refrigerate for 1 hour.

Heat the oil and remaining stick of butter (enough to reach halfway up the chicken), using 1 or 2 skillets, or fry chicken in batches; the pan shouldn't be crowded. The oil-butter mixture should be fairly hot before you add the chicken, seam side down. Reduce the heat and fry gently until the chicken pieces are golden on one side, about 6 to 7 minutes. Turn gently—do not use a fork or the butter will escape. Fry the other side till golden brown, about 5 to 6 minutes more. Do not overcook. Drain on paper towels and serve.

If Chicken Kiev is cooked properly, the seasoned butter will spurt out the moment the chicken is cut.

CHICKEN BREASTS WITH SHRIMP

Carrots, onions, cucumbers, and shrimp, with a rich egg-yolk wine sauce, complement the chicken breasts.

Serves 3

Salt and pepper	1 bay leaf
6 chicken breast halves, with	1-1/2 cups chicken stock
wing attached	1-1/2 cups dry white wine
Cooking oil	1 or 2 cucumbers, peeled,
1 medium-sized onion, peeled	seeded, and diced
and sliced	1 cup raw peeled shrimp
1 or 2 cloves garlic, minced	4 egg yolks
3 sprigs parsley	1/4 cup milk or cream
1 carrot, scraped and diced	

Season the chicken well and brown on all sides in hot oil. Pour off excess fat and add the onion, garlic, parsley, carrot, bay leaf, stock, and wine. Bring to a boil, cover, and reduce the heat to simmer the chicken until tender, about 45 minutes.

Discard the bay leaf and parsley. Add the cucumbers and simmer, uncovered, for 5 minutes, adding the shrimp after about 2 to 3 minutes. They should simmer no more than 2 minutes or so.

Arrange the chicken breasts in pairs, back to back, on a suitable platter. Scoop out the shrimps and vegetables and put them on top of the chicken; keep warm. In a saucepan beat together the egg yolks and milk or cream. In a thin stream, gradually add the pan liquids, beating continuously. Return to a very gentle heat only long enough for the sauce to thicken, stirring constantly. Correct the seasoning. The sauce must not boil again, or it will curdle. Pour the sauce over the chicken to serve.

ISLAND CHICKEN

Here is a rich Caribbean chicken—the sauce contains green bananas, mushrooms, and cream.

Serves 4 to 6

2 green bananas, peeled
1/2 cup rum (dark, preferably)
8 chicken breast halves, boned
   and pounded thin
Salt and pepper
All-purpose flour
1/2 stick (4 tablespoons) butter
2 tablespoons cooking oil

6 shallots, minced
1 cup sliced fresh mushrooms
2 tablespoons green
   peppercorns, drained
1 tablespoon Dijon mustard
1-1/2 cups cream
1 not-too-ripe avocado, peeled
   and sliced (optional)

Slice the bananas diagonally about 1/4 inch thick. Heat half the rum and pour over the bananas to marinate. (This can be done well ahead of time.)

Season the chicken breasts with salt and pepper and dredge in flour, shaking off any excess. Heat 2 tablespoons of the butter and 2 tablespoons cooking oil in a large skillet. Sauté the chicken without browning for about 4 minutes on each side; do not overcook. When you turn the chicken, add the shallots and mushrooms. After a few minutes add the peppercorns. When the chicken is cooked, transfer it to a heated platter and keep warm.

Add remaining 1/4 cup rum to the pan over medium heat, ignite it, and let the flames burn off the alcohol. Deglaze the pan, scraping and stirring. Add the mustard, cream, avocado, and marinated bananas to the sauce and simmer, stirring often, until it has thickened and the bananas are soft but not mushy. Stir in the remaining 2 tablespoons butter and pour the sauce over the chicken. Serve with noodles or rice.

HAWAIIAN CHICKEN

Serves 2 to 3

4 chicken breast halves,
  skinned and boned
1/4 cup cornstarch
3 tablespoons corn oil, more if
  necessary
1 green pepper, seeded and cut
  in 1-inch squares
1 medium-sized onion, peeled
  and cut in about 1-inch wide
  wedges, separated

4 tablespoons chicken stock
1/2 teaspoon salt
1 teaspoon granulated sugar
1 teaspoon soy sauce
2 teaspoons sake or dry sherry
1 small can pineapple chunks,
  drained
1 teaspoon cornstarch dissolved
  in 1 tablespoon water

Cut the chicken in bite-sized cubes. Roll the chicken cubes in 1/4 cup cornstarch so each piece is well coated.

Heat the oil in a large skillet, add the chicken, and cook quickly over medium heat, stirring often, until the meat is opaque and the coating firm but not brown—about 3 to 4 minutes. Remove the chicken and reserve. Add the green pepper and onion to the pan, adding a little more oil if needed; cook, stirring, for 3 minutes.

Combine the chicken stock, salt, sugar, soy sauce, sake, and pineapple. Pour the pineapple sauce into the vegetables, replace the chicken cubes, and heat throughly, tossing. Add the teaspoon of cornstarch with the water, to the pan, and cook the sauce, stirring, until it is thick and clear—about 30 seconds. Serve with either fried or steamed rice.

CHICKEN WITH ASPARAGUS, CHINESE STYLE

Serves 2 to 3

4 chicken breast halves, boned
   and skinned
1 tablespoon soy sauce
2 tablespoons sake or dry
   sherry
1/2 teaspoon honey

1 pound tender asparagus
2 tablespoons cooking oil
1/2 cup water
1 clove garlic, minced
2 tablespoons soybean paste

Cut the chicken breasts into 1/2-inch cubes. Pour the soy sauce, sake or sherry, and the honey over the chicken and reserve.

Cut the woody part off the asparagus and discard. "Roll-cut" the stalk of the asparagus diagonally, to get the maximum cooking surface, into 1/2-inch-long slices. Leave the tips uncut.

Heat a wok or skillet over high heat until hot, add the oil, swirl, and let it heat about 30 seconds or so. Add, in this order: garlic, soybean paste, and asparagus.

Stir to coat the asparagus with the oil and soybean paste, then add 1/2 cup water and stir. Cover and let the asparagus steam-cook for 2 minutes or so. Uncover, add the marinated chicken, and continue to cook, stirring all the time, about 2 to 3 minutes. Taste for seasoning and serve at once.

SPICY CHINESE CHICKEN

These velvety chicken strips are tossed with hot green pepper,
walnuts, and whole scallions. It's a lovely and tasty light dish.

Serves 2

1-1/2 tablespoons cornstarch
1 egg white
2 large chicken breast halves,
  skinned and boned
5 tablespoons peanut oil
4 whole scallions cut into 2-inch
  pieces, then halved
  lengthwise
1 tablespoon peeled and
  minced fresh ginger

1 hot green Chinese pepper,
  seeded and minced
1/2 cup chopped cashews or
  walnuts
1 tablespoon soy sauce
2 tablespoons dry sherry or
  ginger wine
1 teaspoon granulated sugar

Mix the cornstarch and egg white with your fingers (any other
way would make it frothy). Cut the chicken breasts into strips
against the grain to resemble thin French fries. Combine with the
cornstarch mixture, using your fingers. Heat a wok or skillet until
hot, add 3 tablespoons of the oil, swirl, and heat about 30 seconds.

Toss in the coated chicken and stir-fry, scraping and tossing,
until golden brown and cooked—about 2 to 3 minutes. Reserve.

In another wok or skillet heat the remaining 2 tablespoons oil.
Add the scallions, ginger, and pepper. Stir-fry over high heat for 1
minute. Add the nuts and stir. Add the cooked chicken and
remaining ingredients and stir-fry only long enough to let the
liquid bubble up and reduce a little. Serve immediately.

In the Oven

ROASTED

Here are whole roasted chickens, stuffed or simply flavored, and marinated or sauced chicken pieces—all roasted in an open pan, or sometimes in an uncovered casserole.

There are simple recipes—like the classic Poulet Rôti, Minted Chicken, or a chicken roasted with wine and garlic—and some exotic ones, like the one stuffed with fruits and pine nuts (Persian style), the one that's rubbed with Indian spices, the one that's "fried" in the oven. And among the cut-up chicken recipes, there are sauces from cheese, yogurt, wine, and honey, plus even a lovely ham stock.

All the recipes in this chapter are particularly carefree to do.

TO TRUSS A CHICKEN

Small chickens are so tender that they are easily disjointed or cut into quarters after being roasted. Large chickens or other poultry should be trussed and the wishbone removed, to make carving easier. To truss a bird one needs a trussing needle and string, and a small sharp knife to remove the wishbone. If you are investing in a trussing needle buy the longest possible. The needle should be as long as the bird is wide, but if it is longer it can take care of future needs and larger fowl. Use only natural-colored string, since dyed string will "bleed." The string must be thin enough to go through the eye of the needle and strong enough to hold the shape of the bird during cooking. The wishbone is removed before cooking, so that the white meat may be sliced diagonally away from the carver without encountering the obstacle of bones. The trussing is done for the appearance or presentation of the bird, as well as to make carving easier by pushing the legs down further and exposing more of the white meat.

REMOVING THE WISHBONE

Place the chicken on its back, legs facing you. Fold back excess skin from the neck down toward the legs. With the left hand locate the wishbone, between the neck and breastbone. Holding a sharp, pointed knife in the right hand, cut and scrape all along the bone until it can be removed.

TRUSSING THE CHICKEN

With the bird in the same position, spread the wings, one at a time, and chop off the first two joints. Lift one of the chicken legs up in the air, forcing it back, to break the hip and knee joints. Repeat with the other leg. Now, with the legs in the original position but stretched down as far as possible, the chicken is ready to be trussed.

Insert the trussing needle through the stretched-down left leg, leaving 3 to 4 inches of string. Fold the skin to close the opening and take a stitch through it to secure it shut. Insert the needle through the other leg, also stretched down, the same way as the first. Bring the string up to the wing on the same side. Fold excess skin from the neck over the backbone. Turn the chicken over, back side up, and stitch from the first wing through the excess neck skin and backbone and through the second wing to force both wings back. Tie the ends of the string. The chicken is now trussed.

A stuffed chicken is trussed in the same way.

TO ROAST A CHICKEN

The white meat, the breast, of a chicken is the most desirable part, although a lot of people, and I'm one of them, will argue that it is also the driest part. (That is why we argue.) Care must be taken during roasting not to dry the meat out. This can be achieved by covering the breasts during cooking with slices of salt pork, thick rashers of bacon, a "beauty paste" of melted butter, seasoned or not and used for frequent basting, or a loose covering of aluminum foil. All coverings—bacon, foil, etc.—must be removed before the end of the roasting time to let the skin brown. If the chicken is to be roasted uncovered, it should be roasted first on one side, then on the other side for part of the cooking period. Only during the final part of the cooking should the bird lie on its back, the breast browning. This method will also protect the tenderer white meat from getting too dry.

If the roasting is done in a covered pot, like a clay pot, or a covered roasting pan, even though it is cooked in the oven it is *not* roasting. Moisture is allowed to build up in any well-covered pan, and the result is oven steaming, not roasting. (All such recipes for whole chickens can be found in the first section of the casserole chapter.)

For roasting a chicken, the oven must be preheated and the chicken should be roasted at a high temperature for the first 10 minutes to allow the skin to firm and so seal in the juices, flavor, and nutrients. The rest of the time the chicken should be roasted at a moderate temperature. It should be allowed to sit for 10 minutes before being carved, and if the chicken is to be used cold, it should be carved when cold. This rest will allow the juices to be retained in the chicken. A chicken is "done" when a skewer or fork is inserted in the thickest part of the thigh and the juices run clear, not pink, or when a meat thermometer inserted in the thickest part of the thigh measures an internal temperature of 190 degrees.

TO STUFF A CHICKEN

Never stuff a bird until just before cooking. The inside and outside temperature of stuffed chicken will vary a great deal even under refrigeration. The inside may spoil while the outside still smells fresh. There is no detecting this until the chicken is carved and the stuffing extracted. The stuffing can be made ahead of time, but it should only be placed in the cavity just before cooking.

If the chicken or turkey is large enough, two stuffings may be used—one in the neck cavity, the other in the carcass.

A bird is stuffed for two reasons. The first is to flavor and moisten the fowl, the other to make it go further. There is no reason why both can't be achieved at the same time. The flavor comes mostly from fats, such as ground pork or rendered bacon or chicken fat. The bulk can be bread crumbs or bread cubes, rice, noodles, or other starches. Prunes, raisins, and stock or milk will moisten the stuffing.

Do not overstuff a chicken. The stuffing will swell during cooking, especially if bread or rice is part of it. A 2-1/2-pound chicken holds about 2 cups of stuffing. A larger one holds approximately 1 cup of stuffing per pound of chicken.

WHOLE CHICKENS

POULET RÔTI

If you are able to buy a chicken from a farmer, or any private source that will give you a decent bird, roast it the classic way at least once and you may never want it any other way again.

1 roasting chicken	Fresh tarragon
Salt and freshly ground pepper	Unsalted butter

Season the cavity of the chicken with salt, freshly ground pepper, 2 or 3 sprigs of fresh tarragon, and about 3 tablespoons of unsalted butter.

Truss the chicken. Cover the outside with a paste of *unsalted* butter. (Salt extracts moisture and the chicken won't get as crisp.) Roast the chicken on its back in an oven preheated to 450 degrees for 10 to 12 minutes, then turn it on one side, reduce the oven temperature to 350, and continue to roast. Turn and baste the chicken frequently until it is done and brown and crisp. A 3- to 4-pound chicken will take approximately 1 hour and 15 minutes.

During the time the chicken is in the oven, make a simple stock with the tips of the wings, the neck, the giblets, a small onion, salt, a few peppercorns, and water to cover. Simmer 1 hour. Strain.

Transfer the chicken to a platter when it is done and deglaze the pan over high heat with the stock, stirring and scraping. Taste for seasoning. A tablespoon or two of dry vermouth may be added to the gravy.

ROAST CHICKEN WITH BACON

*One of the simplest of roasting recipes—using a latticework of
bacon to protect the chicken.*

Serves 4 or 5

Seasoning: this may include   1 roasting hen, 4 to 5 pounds
   garlic or herbs, or both   1/2 pound bacon in slices

Season the inside of the chicken. Cook 1 slice of bacon in the
roasting pan on top of the stove. Add the chicken. Use the rest of
the bacon to cover the top of the chicken, weaving the strips
lengthwise and crosswise—this way the bacon won't slip off.

Bake in a preheated 375-degree oven for 40 minutes, then lift
off the bacon and reserve. Continue to bake the chicken, basting it
at times, until the chicken tests done and the thigh bones feel
loose—about 45 minutes more. Serve the bacon with the chick-
en—it's delicious.

MINTED CHICKEN

A simple roast chicken flavored with the wonderful taste of mint.

Serves 2 or 3

Salt and pepper
1 whole fryer
2 tablespoons butter

1 bunch fresh mint, rinsed and
    dried
1 teaspoon dried mint

Season the inside of the chicken and rub the outside with the butter. Place the bunch of fresh mint in the cavity of the chicken. Roast in a preheated 375-degree oven, allowing approximately 20 minutes per pound. Baste occasionally. Five or 10 minutes before the chicken is done, sprinkle the top with dried mint. Serve with mint sauce on the side.

ROAST CHICKEN STUFFED WITH SHRIMP

Serves 4

1 roasting chicken, about 4
  pounds
Salt and pepper
3 teaspoons dried tarragon
8 slices white bread (French is
  best)
1 cup light cream
1/2 stick (4 tablespoons) butter

2 tablespoons chopped shallots
2 eggs, well beaten
Juice of 1 lemon
1 cup cooked peas
1 to 2 cups cooked shrimp,
  chopped
4 slices bacon

Salt and pepper the inside of the chicken and sprinkle 1 teaspoon of the tarragon into the cavity. Set aside while you prepare
the stuffing.

Toast the bread in a slow oven to make it as dry as possible.
When it is cool enough to handle, break it into crumbs into a bowl.
Let the crumbs soak with the cream for half an hour. Melt the
butter in a saucepan and sauté the shallots lightly, about 5
minutes. Add the bread crumb mixture to the saucepan and cook
for about 5 minutes, stirring constantly. Cool slightly. Add all the
other ingredients except the bacon, season, and stir well. Stuff the
cavity of the chicken with this mixture. Close the cavity with
toothpicks or skewers, then truss the chicken if you wish. Any
excess stuffing can be baked separately in a small, covered casserole.

Cover the breast of the chicken with bacon and bake in a
preheated oven at 375 degrees for 35 minutes. Remove the bacon
and continue to bake until the chicken is done and golden brown,
about 40 minutes more. Serve with a green salad.

ROAST CHICKEN STUFFED WITH NOODLES

Serves 6

3 to 4 cups cooked noodles
1 cup diced ham, salami, or
   fried bacon, etc.
1 cup grated or crumbled
   cheese, strong if you like it
1/3 cup cream or milk

1 clove garlic, peeled and
   crushed
2 whole fryers, about 3 pounds
   each
Salt and pepper

Combine the noodles, ham, cheese, milk or cream, and garlic. Season the insides of the chickens with salt and pepper, removing and reserving any chicken fat. Stuff both cavities with this mixture, close the openings with toothpicks or skewers, and season the outsides. Place any lumps of chicken fat on the breasts to protect and baste the white meat with, or spread a little butter over them. Roast the chickens in a preheated 375-degree oven for 1-1/2 hours, or until the chickens are done. Baste often to crisp the skin.

PERSIAN CHICKEN

Here the chicken is stuffed with fruits and nuts, which are later mixed with rice. A sumptuous dish.

Serves 4

1 large onion, finely chopped
1/4 cup cooking oil
1 cup chopped apricots, fresh, dried, or canned
1/2 cup prunes, chopped
1 or 2 tart green apples, cored but not peeled, and diced
1/2 cup raisins
1/2 cup currants
1/2 cup pine nuts

1 teaspoon ground cinnamon
1 teaspoon dried tarragon
Salt and freshly ground pepper
1 roasting chicken, 4 to 5 pounds
Garlic powder
4 cups cooked rice (use a pinch of saffron to color the rice yellow when cooking it)

Sauté the onion in the oil until limp and very tender, about 10 to 15 minutes. Add the fruits, nuts, and spices; season with salt and pepper. Sauté this mixture over very low heat for 20 minutes, then cool it a little and place it in the cavity of the chicken. Fasten the opening with skewers or toothpicks. Season the outside of the chicken with salt and a little garlic powder.

Bake in a preheated 400-degree oven for 15 minutes. Baste with accumulated fat, then reduce the temperature to 325 degrees and continue to roast, basting at times, until the chicken is done—about 1-1/4 hours more.

Carve the chicken into serving pieces. Mix the stuffing and any juices off the carving board with the rice. Serve the rice in a suitable dish, topped with the chicken pieces.

ROAST CHICKEN WITH WINE-RAISIN SAUCE

Serves 6

1 cup raisins
1 cup port
2 whole fryers, about 2 to 2-1/2
    pounds each
1/2 stick (4 tablespoons) butter
Salt
2 tablespoons dried tarragon
8 strips larding pork or bacon
1/2 cup Cognac

8 shallots, finely chopped
2 cloves garlic, finely chopped
1 cup red wine
6 juniper berries
1 *bouquet garni*: about 2 sprigs
    parsley, 1/2 bay leaf, 1 sprig
    or 1/8 teaspoon thyme
    wrapped in cheesecloth

Soak the raisins in the port to plump, adding a little water if necessary; reserve. Dry the chickens and rub inside and out with butter, salt, and tarragon. Tie larding pork or bacon over their breasts. Place the chickens in a large casserole and bake, uncovered, in a preheated 425-degree oven until the birds start to color—about 10 minutes. Pour the Cognac over the chickens and ignite. When the flames have died down, add the shallots and garlic, reduce the temperature to 350 degrees, and roast for 20 to 30 minutes, or until the chickens are golden brown.

Remove and discard the bacon or pork. Add the wine, juniper berries, and *bouquet garni* and cook, covered, until the chickens are almost done. Discard the *bouquet garni* and add the reserved raisins and their liquid and bake, uncovered, for the rest of the time; the chickens will take from 1 to 1-1/2 hours to cook. Baste frequently with the pan juices.

STAY-AT-HOME CHICKEN

A simple covered, then uncovered, garlic and wine chicken. Save the garlic if you'd like to use it again—see page 36 and page 40.

Serves 2 or 3

4 heads garlic cloves, peeled   1 whole broiler or fryer
   but uncut   1 cup dry white wine
Salt and pepper

Lay the garlic cloves on the bottom of a casserole. Season the chicken inside and out, then place it on the bed of garlic and add the wine. Bake, covered, at 400 degrees for 30 minutes, then uncover and baste. Bake, uncovered, for 30 more minutes, or until the chicken is brown and done. Baste occasionally.

Strain the garlic and freeze in a plastic bag to use again. Carve the chicken and serve the wine sauce on the side.

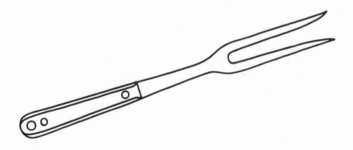

CHICKEN TANDOORI

A variation on the famous Indian chicken; here the chicken is marinated in a spicy paste overnight, then roasted.

Serves 2 or 3

1 dried red chili pepper,
   crushed
1 teaspoon paprika
1 teaspoon turmeric
1/2 teaspoon freshly ground
   black pepper

1 teaspoon salt
1 teaspoon peanut oil
1 teaspoon vinegar
1 fryer, about 3 pounds
Cooking oil

Combine the chili pepper, paprika, turmeric, pepper, salt, peanut oil and vinegar to make a paste. Rub the chicken inside and out with the paste and, if possible, slip some of it under the skin. Refrigerate overnight. The next day, roast in a pan filmed with some cooking oil in a preheated 400-degree oven until the chicken is tender, about 1 hour. Turn at times to crisp the chicken evenly.

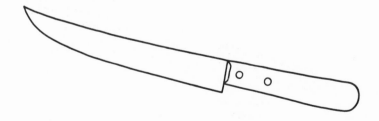

CHICKEN IN "CLAY"

Though roasted, the chicken is protected by a wrapping of flour, salt and water, really a pot in itself.

Serves 2 or 3

4 cups all-purpose flour
1 cup salt (yes, 1 cup)
2 cups water

1 whole fryer, about 3 pounds, rinsed and dried

Combine the flour, salt, and water: this is known as "baker's clay." Roll out the clay large enough to wrap the chicken. Place the rolled-out dough in an ungreased baking pan. Put the chicken on the dough and wrap the dough around the chicken completely, so no juices will escape during cooking. The dough may be decorated to look like a hen.

Roast in a preheated 400-degree oven for 1-1/2 hours, then serve hot. A hammer and chisel or an old knife are needed to lift the top off the clay. The chicken is served from the lower half in its own juice. The clay is discarded.

CHICKEN "FRIED" WHOLE

A whole chicken is coated and then roasted in oil—to give a "Maryland fried" crispness to the skin.

Serves 2 or 3

1 fryer, about 3 pounds
Cooking oil
1 egg

2 cups unseasoned bread
  crumbs
1 teaspoon salt
1 teaspoon curry powder

Rinse and dry the chicken. Skewer the opening shut with toothpicks or skewers. Combine and beat together the egg and 1/4 cup oil in a wide bowl. In a large plastic bag combine the bread crumbs, salt, and curry powder. Dip the chicken in the egg mixture until it is well covered all over, using a pastry brush if necessary. Transfer the chicken to the bag containing the bread crumb mixture; shake the bag so that the chicken becomes as well covered with crumbs as possible.

Preheat the oven to 375 degrees. Pour enough cooking oil into a baking pan to cover the bottom by 1/8 inch. Heat the oil in the oven, and when it is hot place the chicken on its side in the oil and cook, turning it at times, until it is crisp and done—about 50 minutes to 1 hour.

CHICKEN PIECES

CHICKEN IN SCALLION-CHEESE SAUCE

Serves 4

2 broilers, halved
Salt and pepper
1/2 stick (4 tablespoons) butter
1/2 cup all-purpose flour
3 cups milk, more if needed,
heated

1 cup grated Parmesan
2 tablespoons Durkee's sauce
2 teaspoons Dijon-type
mustard
10 small whole scallions,
chopped

Season the broilers on both sides. Lay, skin side up, in a pan just large enough to hold the chickens in one layer. Roast at 375 degrees until the chicken is almost done, 50 or 60 minutes.

During this time make the sauce. Melt the butter in a large saucepan. Add the flour and cook over low heat, stirring constantly, until the roux is in one ball. Remove from the heat and add the hot milk all at once, beating vigorously with a wire whisk. Return to low heat and add the cheese, Durkee's sauce, mustard, and 1/2 teaspoon salt. Stir and cook about 2 minutes, until the sauce is smooth and thick. Pour the cheese sauce over the chicken, top with the scallions, and bake until the cheese is bubbly and the chicken is done.

ROASTED CHICKEN PIECES WITH CHEESE AND BACON

Serves 3

Salt and pepper
1 fryer, cut into serving pieces
Bacon

Slices of mozzarella or Swiss
cheese

Season the chicken on both sides and spread the pieces in a shallow baking pan, skin side down. Bake for 30 minutes at 350 degrees. Turn the chicken and cover each piece with bacon. Return the pan to the oven and bake for 20 minutes or more, or until the chicken is done and the bacon crisp. Just before serving, lift the bacon off the chicken, cover each piece with a slice of cheese, replace the bacon, and roast only long enough for the cheese to melt.

CHICKEN WITH LOW-CALORIE YOGURT

Serves 4 to 6

4 to 6 pounds chicken pieces or
    2 fryers in serving pieces
Salt and pepper
Butter
2 cloves garlic, put through a
    garlic press

3 cups low-calorie yogurt
1 to 2 tablespoons Dijon-type
    mustard, or to taste
1 bunch chives or thin scallions,
    chopped

Season the chicken pieces on all sides. Butter an oven-to-table baking pan lightly. Put in the chicken pieces, skin side down, scatter the crushed garlic around, and bake at 400 degrees for 15 to 20 minutes. Turn the chicken pieces so the skin side is up. Continue to bake until the chicken is done, about 30 minutes more.

Combine the yogurt, mustard, and chives or scallions. Drain all the fat from the pan, smother the chicken with the yogurt mixture, and bake for 5 minutes more, till the yogurt is good and hot.

HONEY CHICKEN

Chicken pieces marinated in honey, brandy, and fresh ginger are baked in the marinade.

Serves 4

Salt and pepper	1/2 cup brandy
2 fryers, each 2-1/2 pounds, cut	3 tablespoons honey
into serving pieces (boned	1 tablespoon peeled and
optional)	minced fresh ginger
OR 8 chicken breast halves	
(boned optional)	

Season the chicken on both sides. Place in one layer in a baking pan. Combine the brandy, honey, and ginger and pour the mixture over the chicken. Leave to marinate anywhere from 1 hour at room temperature to several hours refrigerated. Turn at times.

Roast the chicken, with its marinade, in a preheated 400-degree oven until done, turning the chicken once or twice; it should finish cooking with the skin side up to allow the skin to get crisp. Boned chicken will take about 30 minutes to cook, with bone in 40 minutes.

SHARON'S CHICKEN IN RED WINE

Serves 3

1 fryer, cut into serving pieces
Salt and pepper
1 stick (1/4 pound) butter, at
    room temperature
1/2 teaspoon dried tarragon

1/4 teaspoon dried basil
1/2 teaspoon summer savory
1 tablespoon finely chopped
    shallots
Dry red wine

Place the chicken in a shallow baking dish, and season with salt and pepper to taste. Mix together the butter, tarragon, basil, summer savory, and shallots and coat the top of the chicken. Pour red wine down the side of the dish until it comes halfway up the chicken.

Bake, uncovered, for 40 minutes or until browned, in a preheated 400-degree oven. If prepared early in the day and kept in the refrigerator, bring to room temperature before cooking.

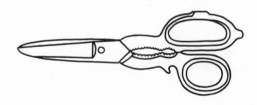

SHOW BIZ CHICKEN (PART HAM)

Broilers, split, are roasted in a ham stock with onions, mushrooms, garlic and ham—an earthy and delicious way to do them.

Serves 6

1 ham bone or ham hock	1 cup diced fresh mushroom
5 to 6 cups water	stems
1 cup diced ham	2 to 3 cloves garlic, minced
1 cup diced onion	3 broilers, split
	Salt
	Liquid mint sauce

Boil the ham bone or ham hock in 5 to 6 cups water for at least 1 hour and then reduce the liquid by fast boiling to 2 cups.

Spread the ham, onions, mushroom stems, and garlic over the bottom of a large baking pan. Place the broiler halves, skin down, in a single layer over the mixture. Season lightly, since the ham is salty. Pour the hot ham stock over the chicken and roast at 400 degrees for 15 to 20 minutes. Turn the chicken over and continue to roast until the chicken is done and the skin crisp. Baste 2 or 3 times during baking.

Pour a little mint sauce over the chicken about 5 minutes before removing from the pan. Place the chicken on a serving dish and pour the pan juices and bits on top.

CHICKEN IN BREAD "BOXES"

Here a sour-cream and curry coating flavors "fried" roasted chicken pieces; the "boxes" are made of toasted bread.

Serves 4 to 6

2 fryers, cut into small serving
    pieces
2 cups sour cream
1 teaspoon curry powder
1/2 teaspoon dry mustard
1 large clove garlic, peeled and
    crushed (optional)

1 tablespoon salt
Unflavored bread crumbs
2 loaves stale white bread,
    unsliced
Cooking oil

Dry the chicken on paper towels. In a large bowl combine the sour cream, curry powder, mustard, and garlic. Stir the chicken pieces in this mixture until well coated. Combine the bread crumbs and salt in a plastic bag. Drop the chicken pieces, one at a time, into the bag and shake until well coated. Spread on waxed paper to dry for at least 1 hour.

TO MAKE THE "BOXES"

Meanwhile, hollow out the loaves of stale white bread—cut about two-thirds of the way down the loaf about 1 inch from the edge, and keep cutting horizontally till the section comes free. Repeat with the second loaf. Toast the "boxes" lightly in a preheated 300-degree oven for about 10 minutes. Remove from the oven and reserve.

Turn the oven heat up to 400 degrees. Cover the bottom of 1 or 2 baking pans, as needed, with cooking oil and heat the oil on top of the range. Add chicken pieces in one layer and transfer the pan to the oven. Cook until done, turning the chicken often to crisp and brown the pieces evenly—about 45 minutes. Fill the "boxes," which will absorb excess fat, and serve.

CHICKEN PIÑA COLADA

Serves 4

4 pounds chicken pieces
Salt and freshly ground black
   pepper
1 16-ounce can cream of
   coconut

1 8-ounce can pineapple
   chunks, drained, or 1 cup
   chopped
6 slices bacon

Season the chicken on both sides and place in 1 layer in an oven-to-table dish. Pour the cream of coconut over the chicken and distribute the pineapple chunks over the top. Cover with slices of bacon and bake at 400 degrees until the chicken is tender, about 1 hour and 10 minutes.

CHICKEN JERKY

Serves 4 for hors d'oeuvres

4 chicken breast halves,
   skinned and boned
1/4 cup soy sauce

2 tablespoons dry sherry
1 clove garlic, peeled and
   crushed

Freeze the chicken a little till firm—it will be easier to slice. Then cut the breast halves into strips *with* the grain, as long as possible and about 1/4 inch thick. Combine the remaining ingredients and pour over the chicken strips. Marinate at room temperature for 3 or 4 hours, stirring occasionally. Place the strips a little apart on a rack in a very low oven (200 degrees) for about 2 hours. The chicken should be fairly hard and "chewy." Cool before serving.

Over an Open Fire

GRILLED OR BROILED

Starting with Chicken au Pistou, for that time in late summer when fresh basil is abundant, here is a small but excellent selection of recipes for the grill or broiler. Some of the chickens are marinated or covered with seasonings, and some are broiled plain to be served with elegant, unusual sauces. Tastes include snail butter, mustard and garlic, parsley, peanut butter, curry. . . .

TO BARBECUE A CHICKEN

The secret lies in the right kind of fire, not in the right kind of grill. One universal rule to follow on every grill is to allow about 1-inch thickness of glowing coals for 12 to 17 minutes perfect cooking time.

Start the coals about 1 hour before grilling, although the correct time will depend on the fire starter and the amount of coals used. You should begin grilling only when the coals are covered with gray ash. And adding coals or wood to a fire during the cooking time will cool the fire and affect the regularity of the heat—don't do it. Make a proper bed of coals first.

Fat drippings from the chicken will make the coals blaze and cause the chicken to dry up and shrink. To extinguish flareups caused by these drippings, use a water pistol or a baster filled with water. Both will direct the water accurately to the coals, rather than wash off any seasoning from the chicken on the grill. Or, if your grill boasts a lid, replace it to extinguish any flareup.

Flat pieces of boned chicken are best cooked on an open grill, just a few minutes to each side. The chicken pieces should be well covered with sauce or marinade to prevent the meat from becoming too dry.

A whole chicken, especially a large one, is best cooked over a drip tray (indirect heat), with a lid or aluminum foil covering. Either would allow moisture to build up, again preventing the chicken from getting dry. It would also cut down cooking time and save coals.

CHICKEN AU PISTOU

For a magnificent, unusual treat, broil the chickens with the famous Provençal basil paste between the meat and skin.

Serves 4

1/2 cup chopped fresh Italian parsley	1/4 cup pine nuts
	4 to 6 cloves garlic, peeled
1 cup chopped fresh sweet basil, pressed down	Olive oil
	2 broilers, split
1/4 cup grated Parmesan	Salt and pepper

Combine the parsley, basil, Parmesan, pine nuts, and garlic. Make a paste of it, either by blending it a few seconds in an electric blender, with about 3 tablespoons of olive oil, or by pounding it in a mortar and pestle, stirring in enough olive oil to make the paste smooth—do not make it too mushy.

Flatten the broiler halves a little between waxed paper with the broad side of a heavy knife. Carefully separate some of the skin from the chicken and insert the *pistou* between the skin and the chicken, saving a little. Brush both sides of the chicken with olive oil and season, then smear the remaining *pistou* along the insides of the chickens.

Broil for 20 minutes skin side down, then turn and broil the other side until the chickens are tender and crisp, about 15 to 20 minutes more. Baste once or twice with olive oil after turning the chickens to make the skin good and crisp.

CHICKEN DIABLE

A garlic-mustard marinade makes this chicken crisp and pungent.

Serves 2

1 broiler, split
4 large cloves garlic, puréed

6 to 8 tablespoons Dijon-style mustard

Rub the garlic purée all over the chicken, putting any bits that fall off into the mustard. Then smear the chicken with the mustard. Marinate for 1 hour.

Barbecue or broil the chicken until done, starting skin side down and turning every once in a while. It will take about 30 to 40 minutes.

BARBECUED CHICKEN BASTED WITH LEMON SAUCE

Serves 4

2 broilers, split
Salt
2 lemons, halved
1 stick butter (optional)

2 tablespoons dried tarragon
3/4 teaspoon lemon pepper
    marinade

Season the broilers on both sides with salt. Squeeze the lemons and reserve the juice. Melt the butter in a small saucepan. Add the lemon juice, tarragon, and marinade.

Brush the chickens with the lemon butter, then place them, meat side down, on the grill. Put the lemon butter near the grill to keep warm, and brush it on the chickens often, turning them also to crisp the skin. Cooking time will depend on the heat of the coals, though a rough estimate is about 30 to 40 minutes in all.

SPICY PEANUT-BUTTERED CHICKEN

Serves 4 to 6

1/4 cup peanut oil
3 to 5 hot dried chili peppers
4 pounds chicken pieces

1 cup peanut butter
1 cup catsup

Heat the peanut oil to medium hot in a small saucepan. Crush the chili peppers into the oil and heat together for about 3 to 5 minutes. Drain and discard the chilies. Brush both sides of the chicken pieces with the spicy oil. Add the rest of the ingredients to the remaining oil and grill or broil the chicken pieces, turning them often and then basting with the peanut sauce. They should be done in about 30 minutes.

AT A SNAIL'S PACE

Broiled chicken served with a lovely hot garlic butter sauce flavored with snails.

Serves 2

Salt and pepper
1 broiler, split
1 stick (1/4 pound) butter
3 tablespoons minced parsley
3 tablespoons minced chives or
   scallions

2 to 3 cloves garlic, peeled and
   crushed
1 small can snails, rinsed and
   drained on paper towels

Season the chicken on both sides and grill or broil in the usual manner until done—about 30 to 40 minutes.

About 5 minutes before the chicken is done, make the sauce: In a saucepan over low heat combine and thoroughly heat the butter, parsley, chives or scallions, garlic, and snails—do not let the butter brown. Transfer the chicken to a heated platter. Pour a little sauce over the chicken and serve the rest separately.

CHICKEN WITH PARSLEY SAUCE

An unusual, creamy parsley sauce and crisp-fried parsley sprigs accompany this broiled chicken.

Serves 2

1 broiler, split	1 cup good chicken stock
Salt and pepper	2 egg yolks
The juice of 2 lemons	1 cup cream
2 tablespoons butter	1 cup chopped parsley
2 tablespoons all-purpose flour	Fried Parsley (see page 105)

Season the chicken on both sides with salt and pepper. Place under the broiler and sprinkle with lemon juice periodically, turning once.

While the chicken is cooking make the sauce. Melt the butter in a saucepan and add the flour. Stir and cook the roux over low heat, without browning, for 2 or 3 minutes. Meanwhile, heat the chicken stock in a separate pan. Remove the roux from the heat and add the stock all at once, beating vigorously with a whisk. Return to low heat and cook, stirring constantly, until the sauce is reduced by half. Beat the egg yolks with a whisk, add the cream, and continue to beat for about 2 minutes. Take the stock sauce off the heat and pour it into the egg mixture while beating briskly. Add the chopped parsley. Remove from the heat and reserve.

When the chicken is done, heat the sauce over low heat, stirring constantly with a wooden spoon, until the sauce is hot and has thickened. Do not boil.

Transfer the chicken to a heated platter, skin side up. Pour the sauce over the chicken and decorate with fried parsley.

FRIED PARSLEY
Cooking oil
1 bunch parsley, washed and
    completely dry
Salt

Heat about 1 inch of oil in a skillet and fry a few sprigs of parsley at a time until crisp—it will take just a second or two. Drain on paper towels and salt well.

MINIATURE CHICKEN KEBABS

A Chinese style kebab.

Makes 4 to 6 small skewers

1/4 cup soy sauce
1/2 cup gin
1/2 teaspoon granulated sugar

3 chicken breast halves, boned
    and cut into 3/4-inch cubes
6 to 8 whole scallions, both
    greens and bulbs cut into
    1-inch pieces

Combine the soy sauce, gin, and sugar. Marinate the cubed chicken for at least 1 hour at room temperature, or for several hours in the refrigerator.

String alternate pieces of chicken and clusters of scallion slices onto bamboo sticks or skewers—about 3 chicken cubes to a skewer. Grill or broil them about 7 to 10 minutes, turning and basting them with the marinade.

CHICKEN SATAY

Chicken Satay is sold in Singapore by street vendors. A curry paste is rubbed into strips of boned chicken, which are grilled and then served with a rich peanut sauce.

Serves 8

12 chicken breast halves, boned	1 tablespoon ground ginger
	1 tablespoon turmeric
2 medium-sized onions, minced	1/2 cup brown sugar
	1 teaspoon salt
3 tablespoons Madras curry powder	Peanut Sauce (see page 107)

Skin the chicken breasts and boil the skin for 30 minutes in sufficient water. (Meanwhile freeze the chicken breasts so they will be easier to slice.) Cool the skin before cutting. Then slice the skin and then the chicken against the grain into 1/4-inch-wide strips. Reserve.

Mix with your hands in a large bowl the onions, curry powder, ginger, turmeric, sugar, and salt. After a few minutes of vigorous mixing it will form a paste. Add the chicken and skin and turn and press the strips with the paste for several minutes, or until both skin and meat are well covered.

On bamboo sticks (you will need 2 to 3 packets of them), alternately string chicken and skin as though sewing, so that each stick holds about 2 or 3 inches of chicken. This can be done ahead of time. Brush some oil from the peanut sauce (see below) over the chicken and grill or broil (or bake in a shallow pan in a 350-degree oven). Turn and baste the chicken strips again after 5 minutes of cooking. Serve with the rest of the peanut sauce as an hors d'oeuvre or with rice and peanut sauce as a main course.

PEANUT SAUCE

1 medium-sized onion, minced	2 tablespoons cayenne pepper
3 tablespoons brown sugar	3/4 cup peanut oil
2 teaspoons salt	2 cups chopped peanuts
1 tablespoon paprika	2 cups plus 1 tablespoon water

Mix vigorously with your hands the onion, sugar, salt, spices, and the 1 tablespoon of water.

Heat the oil in a heavy pan and add the onion mixture, stirring to blend. Add the peanuts all at once and the rest of the water slowly. Continue stirring, then cover and cook on a very low flame for about 10 minutes or until the oil rises to the top. Skim it off and use it to baste the chicken.

The sauce should be kept hot. Before serving, skim off any remaining oil.

CHICKEN IN A NEST

A dish to be made ahead of time and finished under the broiler.
The chickens are simmered, then boned, and nested in spinach
with a garlic-cheese sauce on top.

Serves 6

2 small chickens, about 2 to
   2-1/2 pounds each
1-1/2 medium-sized onions
1 carrot
2 stalks celery
Salt and pepper
3 cups water

1 cup instant-blending flour
1 cup grated mozzarella
1/4 cup dry sherry
1 pound fresh spinach, rinsed
   well
2 cloves garlic
A little milk

Simmer, covered, the chicken, 1 onion, the carrot, celery, some salt and pepper, and the water. Cool the chicken in the broth.

In an electric blender, mix 2-1/2 cups of the chicken broth, half an onion, flour, cheese, sherry, salt, and pepper. Blend until smooth.

Skin and bone the chicken. Cut it into bite-sized pieces and add the sauce. Bring to a boil over a low flame, stirring constantly to avoid sticking. Reserve.

Blend the spinach, garlic, milk, and salt and pepper in the electric blender. Place the chicken in the center of a shallow oven-to-table serving dish with a ring of the puréed spinach around it, like a nest. This may be done ahead of time. Right before serving, broil for several minutes until golden brown.

To End Up Cold

From simple but unusual recipes such as the Spanish vinegar-flavored chicken, the Chinese Drunken Chicken, and the Asiatic walnut-sauced chicken to such elegant French creations as a whole boned chicken stuffed with pâté and suprêmes de volaille *in aspic, here are wonderful cold chicken dishes. There are others in the two chapters that follow this one, notably some excellent salads made from leftover chicken, but here the object is to prepare the chicken from the beginning to end up cold. Most of the recipes are generous and sophisticated, making them perfect for a buffet.*

CHICKEN ESCABECHE

This Spanish chicken is simmered in flavored oil and vinegar, then cooled.

Serves 2

1 cup cooking oil	1 cup water
1 small broiler, quartered	2 bay leaves
1 very large red onion, peeled and sliced	1 or 2 dried red chili peppers, or to taste
1 cup malt or tarragon vinegar	Salt to taste

Heat the oil in a large skillet and brown the chicken lightly. Add the remaining ingredients and simmer, uncovered, until the chicken is done, about 40 minutes. Cool in the broth, and skim off the fat when it has risen to the top.

Arrange the cooled chicken on a platter and top with the onion slices. Pour some of the liquid over the chicken. This can now be refrigerated, but serve at room temperature, with lemon wedges.

MARGOT'S CHICKEN TARRAGON

Serves 2

1 roasting chicken, 2-1/2
  pounds
1 whole lemon, well pricked
  with fork

1 tablespoon plus 1 teaspoon
  dried tarragon
1 tablespoon butter
Salt and pepper

Wash and dry the chicken. Place the lemon and the 1 tablespoon tarragon in the cavity of the chicken. Melt the butter with
the 1 teaspoon tarragon and a little salt and pepper. Brush the
chicken with this mixture. Bake in a brown-in bag in a roasting pan
as per directions on the bag for 1 hour. Cool in the bag and serve at
room temperature.

DRUNKEN CHICKEN

*This Chinese sherry-steeped chicken would be good as an hors
d'oeuvre.*

Serves 2 or 3

1 broiler or small fryer
Water
1 medium-sized onion, halved
Salt and pepper

1 medium-sized fresh ginger
  root, peeled and cut into
  large chunks
1 bottle dry sherry or ginger
  wine

Place the chicken in a heavy pot. Add water to cover, the onion,
and salt and pepper; bring to a boil slowly, then cover and simmer
over low heat for 30 minutes. Let it stand, still covered, for 10
more minutes.

Lift the chicken from the broth and place it, breast side down, in a deep dish, just large enough to hold the chicken. Add the ginger root and sherry or wine and refrigerate for a minimum of 24 hours. Drain and serve the chicken in small pieces cold.

The ginger root and sherry can be used for other Chinese dishes. The chicken stock, of course, has numerous other uses.

CIRCASSIAN CHICKEN

I learned this dish while living in Turkey—it involves a walnut cream sauce poured over boned, simmered chicken. It should be served at room temperature.

Serves 6 to 8

1 stewing hen, 5 to 6 pounds
2 medium-sized onions, quartered
3 carrots, scraped and quartered
3 stalks celery, halved
3 sprigs parsley
2 cloves garlic, chopped

12 peppercorns
Salt
1 pound walnuts, ground in an electric blender
2 tablespoons sweet Hungarian paprika
1/2 cup whipping cream

Place the chicken in a heavy casserole and cover with cold water. Add the onions, carrots, celery, parsley, garlic, and peppercorns and salt. Bring the water to a boil slowly, over low heat, then skim it, cover, and simmer the chicken until tender. Time will depend on age and size. Cool in the broth.

Lift the chicken from the broth and skin and bone it. Tear the meat into bite-sized strips. Spread the chicken pieces in one layer on a serving platter and reserve.

Place the walnuts and paprika in several layers of cheesecloth. Gather the ends and twist and squeeze over a small bowl until the oil from the nuts is squeezed into the bowl. You should get a few tablespoons of red oil—reserve it. If the nuts are dry, skim a little fat off the chicken broth and add it to them before squeezing.

Place the nuts in a saucepan and add 1/2 cup of chicken broth and the cream. Heat gently to lukewarm, stirring often. Spoon over the chicken to cover and dribble the reserved oil on top. Serve at room temperature.

SMOKED CHICKEN

For this recipe it is necessary to own a hickory smoker, but as I have never seen a recipe for smoked chicken in any cookbook, I am including one in this book.

1-1/2 tablespoons coarse salt
   (such as Kosher salt)
1-1/2 tablespoons sugar,
   granulated white or light
   brown

1 teaspoon garlic powder
1 chicken, 3-1/2 to 4 pounds

Combine the salt, sugar, and garlic powder and rub the inside and outside of the chicken with the mixture, slipping some of it under the skin if possible.

Let the chicken rest for 2 hours at room temperature, then place in the smoker and smoke for 8 hours or until completely done—turn at times to let the chicken smoke evenly. Smoking may be done over 2 days, but refrigerate during the night.

Before eating the chicken, refrigerate it at least 24 hours. Carve into thin slices to serve.

TO BONE A CHICKEN

To make a chicken stuffed with pâté or a chicken *galantine* (see following recipes) the chicken must be boned first.

Buy as large a chicken as possible and bring it to room temperature—a very cold fowl is uncomfortable to handle.

Place the chicken on its back with legs facing you. Fold any excess skin from the neck back toward you and with the left hand locate the wishbone. With a small, sharp knife, held against the bone, cut and scrape until the wishbone can be removed.

Spread the wings and chop off the first 2 joints of each. The last bone in the wing remains.

Approach the back of the chicken, the only place where you slit the skin. Turn the chicken so the backbone is up and slit along the apex of the bone the entire length of the chicken, through the skin. Using your left hand to "explore" the obstacles, cut and scrape *against the bone* all the way down one side of the bird, pulling away the flesh and skin as you go. Sever the ball joints at the wing and the second joint, and keep scraping till you come to the ridge of the breast bone. Stop at this point and, starting back again at the backbone, repeat the job on the other side of the carcass, again severing ball joints.

When you arrive again at the ridge of the breastbone, lift the carcass and cut very closely, slowly, against the ridge of the breastbone to free it, being extra careful not to slit the thin skin here.

(If you do puncture the skin at any point, don't panic. Just find a loose piece of skin or a flat piece of meat to cover the hole from the inside, as though patching jeans.)

The upper wing bone remains; but with a little scraping and pulling, you should remove the second joint bones. As for the drumstick bones, I leave them in for the chicken stuffed with pâté, but remove them for the *galantine*. Cut and scrape around both ends and sides, and once they're free pull them out.

CHICKEN STUFFED WITH PÂTÉ

An elegant pâté-stuffed chicken that must be done 2 to 3 days before serving to let the pâté develop its full flavor.

One recipe will serve many at a cocktail party and will serve 6 to 8 sliced as a main course

1 roasting chicken, 5 to 6 pounds	1/2 cup brandy
The fat from the inside of the bird, at least 4 ounces	1/2 pound pork fat, ground
	1 pound veal, ground
1 medium-sized onion, chopped	Salt
3 cloves garlic, chopped	1 teaspoon green peppercorns, mashed
1/2 pound chicken livers	1/2 teaspoon ground allspice
	1/2 teaspoon ground mace

Bone the chicken as described on page 115, leaving the drumstick bone in.

Render the chicken fat in a skillet—if necessary, add butter to make up to 1/2 cup. Add the onion and sauté for about 7 minutes, stirring often. Add the garlic and livers and sauté for 3 to 5 minutes, still stirring. The livers should be brown on the outside, but still pink inside. Pour some of the brandy into an electric blender and add some of the liver mixture. Blend until smooth. Repeat until all the livers are blended. Reserve.

Cook the pork fat in the same skillet until it is brown and crumbly. Add the veal, salt, mashed green peppercorns, allspice, and mace. Sauté until the veal too is cooked.

Combine the liver mixture with the cooked meat and cool. When cool, place some of the pâté in the chicken, starting at the tail end. Sew the chicken as you continue stuffing—this way the chicken can be reconstructed to its original look. (Final wing bones and drumstick bones remain.) Fold the excess skin over the opening at the neck and skewer to prevent the pâté from leaking.

Bake the chicken on its side in a buttered pan for 40 minutes at 350 degrees. Turn the chicken on the other side and bake another 40 minutes. Finish baking the chicken on its back until done— about 40 minutes more.

Refrigerate, covered, for 2 to 3 days before slicing.

CHICKEN GALANTINE

A very elegant creation—a whole boned chicken stuffed with layers of chicken and bacon strips and a spicy sausage, pistachio, and chicken liver mixture.

Serves 8 to 10

1 roasting chicken, 5 to 6
  pounds
1/3 cup brandy
1/4 cup soy sauce
1/2 pound slab bacon
1/4 cup fat from the inside of
  the chicken, or 4 tablespoons
  butter
1/2 pound chicken livers

3 cloves garlic, peeled
1 pound ground chicken or
  turkey meat
1/3 pound spicy sausage meat
1 medium-sized onion, grated
2/3 cup shelled pistachio nuts
2 teaspoons ground allspice
Pepper, and salt only if needed

Bone the chicken as described on page 115, removing the drumstick bones also.

Place the boned chicken, skin side down, on a cutting board. Cut off most of the meat, leaving only about 1/2 inch against the skin. Cut the freed meat into strips as long as possible and 1/2 inch thick, 1/2 inch wide. Combine the brandy and soy sauce and marinate the chicken strips in this mixture.

While the chicken is marinating, cover the slab bacon with cold water and bring to a boil. Discard the water and bring to a boil again with fresh cold water. Simmer over low heat for 1 hour. Discard the water and cool the bacon. Remove the hard skin and cut the bacon into strips similar to the chicken strips. Drain the chicken strips and combine with bacon strips. Reserve the marinade.

Render the chicken fat or heat the butter. Add the chicken livers and sauté them lightly, stirring often.

In an electric blender combine the livers and drippings, the garlic, and the reserved marinade. Blend until smooth. In a bowl combine this liver paste, the ground chicken or turkey, sausage meat, onion, pistachios, allspice, and a liberal grinding of black pepper. Mix it well; this is best done with your hands. Sauté a small amount of this mixture to test the seasoning—correct if necessary.

Lay a bed of the ground mixture inside the chicken, about 2 or 3 inches wide, and filling the drumstick pockets. Sew up the cavity. Place a layer of chicken and bacon strips on top of the mixture. Alternate layers until both mixture and strips have been used up. Sew up the back, fold over the excess neck skin and sew that carefully to the skin.

Tie the *galantine* with string in several places to shape it into a large roll. Surround the chicken with well-buttered aluminum foil and roll it as though working a rolling pin to form a log shape.

Place the *galantine* in a roasting pan in a preheated 425-degree oven and roast for 1 hour. Remove the foil, lower the heat to 375 degrees, and continue to roast for another 1-3/4 to 2 hours. Turn several times during this roasting for uniform color.

Remove the *galantine* to a platter and place another platter on top, with a weight on it. Allow to sit in the refrigerator overnight. Serve the *galantine* chilled, in slices.

SUPRÊMES DE VOLAILLE IN ASPIC

Suprêmes de volaille *are nothing more than boned chicken breasts with a French name. Served in aspic, the dish is as elegant as it sounds and of enormous help to the hostess who likes to cook ahead. It's just as good after a day or two in the refrigerator as it is the day it's made. It can be made in one large mold or in small individual portions. For a crowd, one or two large molds would be easier to cope with, but individual portions are more elegant.*

Serves 8

12 chicken breast halves, boned, skinned, and seasoned

1/2 cup dry white wine or dry champagne (see Aspic; use what you use there)

Aspic (see page 120)

24 very thin slices of pâté, ham, or tongue (OR a mixture of all three)

Slices of hard-boiled eggs, carrots, sprigs of tarragon, and other decorations

Salt and white pepper

Roast the seasoned chicken breasts, slightly overlapping, in a covered casserole, the wine poured on top. The oven should be preheated to 400 degrees. Roast the breasts about 15 minutes, turning them once. Let them cool before you slice them.

Pour the cold, liquid aspic into a well-oiled mold and let it set just a little in the refrigerator. Swirl the mold once or twice to cover the sides with aspic. When the center of the aspic is still liquid but the sides have set, pour the liquid aspic into another bowl. Arrange your decorations on the bottom and sides of the mold. Spoon just a little aspic over the decorations to hold them in place and refrigerate until set. Reserve the liquid aspic at room temperature.

Place cool roasted chicken breasts, one at a time, on a cutting board. Cover with one hand, and with a sharp knife in the other, cut in half horizontally—you now have 24 slices of chicken. Season them lightly with salt and white pepper. Place these, alternating with pâté, ham, or tongue, in a circle on the set aspic in the mold. Cover with the liquid aspic and allow to stand at least 8 hours or overnight in the refrigerator before unmolding.

To unmold: Immerse the mold two-thirds up the side for a moment or two in hot water. Cover with a serving plate and invert. Serve well chilled.

ASPIC
Makes about 5 cups

3 tablespoons (envelopes) unflavored gelatin	4 egg shells
4 egg whites at room temperature	4 cups good chicken stock
	1-1/2 cups dry white wine or dry champagne

Soak the gelatin in a little cold water to soften. Beat the egg whites to soft-peak consistency. Crush the egg shells. Bring the stock to a rolling boil, lower the heat, add the gelatin, and stir until dissolved. Add the beaten egg whites and the shells to the stock. Simmer on low heat for 5 to 7 minutes or until the whites and shells float on the top. Remove from the heat and strain through a colander lined with several thicknesses of cheesecloth. Add the wine or champagne to the clarified aspic. Chill the aspic until cold but still liquid.

CHICKEN COLLÉE

Chicken breast and pâté slices are layered with the velvety sauce collée poured on top.

Serves 4

2 tablespoons butter
3 tablespoons cooking oil
2 cloves garlic, peeled and halved
6 chicken breast halves, skinned and boned

Salt, pepper, and dried tarragon
11 thin slices of pâté (more if needed)
Sauce Collée (see below)
Decorations as desired

Heat the butter, oil, and garlic in a skillet with a well-fitting lid. Season the chicken breasts on both sides with salt, pepper, and tarragon. Sauté the chicken covered, over low heat, until done—about 10 minutes. Turn once during cooking. Remove to a plate, cool, then cover and chill.

When the chicken is cold, cut it horizontally into even slices. Some breasts will cut into 3 slices, most into 2. Arrange alternate chicken and pâté slices in an appropriate dish.

SAUCE COLLÉE
1-1/2 tablespoons (envelopes) unflavored gelatin
2 tablespoons dry vermouth
1/3 cup consommé, undiluted

2 sprigs fresh tarragon
1 cup mayonnaise
1/2 cup sour cream

Soften the gelatin in the vermouth. Heat the consommé and tarragon and add the gelatin mixture to the hot liquid. Stir over low heat until the gelatin has dissolved. Discard the tarragon. Reserve about 3 tablespoons of this mixture for dipping decorations.

Combine the mayonnaise with the sour cream. Beat the gelatin mixture into the mayonnaise a little at the time.

Spoon some of the Sauce Collée over the chicken and pâté. Allow to set in refrigerator. Repeat for a second coating. When set for the second time, dip decorations, such as sprigs of tarragon, slices of carrots or hard-boiled eggs into the reserved *gelée* and arrange in designs on the Chicken Collée. Serve well chilled.

CHICKEN AND LIVER PÂTÉ MOLD

Serves 12 to 14

2 stewing or roasting chickens,
    about 6 pounds each
1 pound bacon, diced
3 stalks celery, halved
2 onions, peeled and quartered
4 sprigs parsley
2 carrots, scraped and halved

2 bay leaves
2 cloves garlic, chopped
Salt and pepper
1 pound of the best liver
    sausage
8 ounces cream cheese
1/4 cup brandy

In a casserole large enough to hold the 2 chickens (or a large skillet for only this step), render the bacon until crisp, remove with a slotted spoon, drain on paper towels, and reserve. Brown the chickens on all sides in the bacon drippings.

Add to the chickens (in a casserole) the celery, onions, parsley, carrots, bay leaves, garlic, salt, and pepper. Cover two-thirds of the way up with cold water. Bring to a boil slowly, then cover, turn the heat very low, and simmer until the chickens are tender. Time will depend on the age of the chickens, but it's generally about 2 hours. Uncover and cool in the broth.

When the chickens are quite cold, slice off all the meat. Reserve good slices and bits separately. Add the reserved bacon to the bits.

Combine the liver sausage, cream cheese, and brandy and beat with an electric beater until smooth.

To assemble, butter a suitable mold and fill with alternating layers of chicken slices, liver mixture, and chicken bits. Cover the mold with foil and weight down well. Refrigerate for 24 to 48 hours. Unmold and serve chilled.

Using What's Already Cooked

Both hot and cold, all these recipes use already cooked chicken. Many of them make very good luncheon dishes, such as the hot Chicken on the Half Shell and the Chicken Quiche or the cold Chicken Salad Niçoise and the Three-Cheese Chicken Pie. In addition, there are two chicken loaves, a croquette recipe, and the popular chicken tacos.

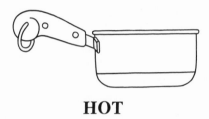

HOT

BAKED AVOCADOS FILLED WITH CHICKEN

Use leftover cooked chicken to stuff tomatoes, eggplant, green peppers, or avocados. The chicken can be made into a salad, the vegetable filled and served cold, or the chicken may be cooked and combined with a sauce, the vegetable filled and baked as in this recipe.

Serves 4

1/2 stick (4 tablespoons) butter
1/4 cup all-purpose flour
1 cup milk, a little more if
    needed
Salt and white pepper
1/2 cup sliced fresh mushrooms
2 tablespoons capers, drained
2 teaspoons Dijon-type
    mustard

2 tablespoons chopped parsley
1-1/2 cups cooked chicken,
    diced
2 very large avocados
1/2 lemon
Grated Parmesan
4 small pats butter

Melt the butter in a saucepan and stir in the flour with a wooden spoon. Cook the roux over low heat for 2 to 3 minutes. Meanwhile heat the milk. Remove the roux from the heat; pour in the hot milk all at once, stirring briskly with a whisk. Return the saucepan to the heat, season, and let it cook a minute or two to thicken. (If it is too thick, add a little more milk.) Add the mushrooms, capers, mustard, parsley, and chicken to the white sauce.

Cut the avocados in half lengthwise. Discard the stones and rub the lemon over the surface to prevent discoloration.

Fill each avocado half with as much of the chicken mixture as it will hold. Sprinkle with a little Parmesan and top with a small pat of butter. Put a cup of boiling water and the lemon halves into a baking dish. Add the avocados and bake in a preheated oven at 375 degrees until the avocados are hot throughout—about 10 minutes.

CHICKEN ON THE HALF SHELL

An elegant luncheon or first-course dish—cheese sauce, sliced chicken, and duxelles *in scallop shells.*

Makes 5 or 6 scallop shells

3-1/2 tablespoons butter
1-1/2 tablespoons all-purpose
    flour
1-1/2 cups light cream or milk,
    hot
5 tablespoons grated Gruyère
1 tablespoon grated Parmesan
Salt and white pepper

1/2 pound fresh mushrooms
6 to 8 scallion bulbs, minced
4 cooked chicken breast halves,
    thinly sliced crosswise
12 small mushroom caps,
    sautéed
1 tablespoon bread crumbs

Melt 1-1/2 tablespoons of the butter in a saucepan and add the flour. Stir with a wooden spoon and cook over low heat for about 2 or 3 minutes without letting the roux brown. Remove the roux from the heat, add the hot cream or milk all at once, beating briskly with a whisk. Return the sauce to low heat and cook, stirring, until it is smooth. Add 2 tablespoons of the Gruyère and the Parmesan cheeses and continue to cook and stir until the cheese has melted and the sauce is thick and smooth. Season to taste and reserve while you make the *duxelles.*

Wash and destem the mushrooms. Dry very well and mince them.

Melt the remaining butter in a heavy skillet. Add the scallions and cook over low heat for about 5 minutes, stirring often. Add the mushrooms and continue to cook and stir for 7 to 10 minutes, until dry. Season liberally.

Pour 1 or 2 tablespoons of cheese sauce into each of 5 or 6 scallop shells. Distribute the sliced chicken evenly among the shells. Spread the *duxelles* over the sliced chicken, then cover with more cheese sauce. Garnish with the sautéed mushroom caps. Combine the remaining grated cheese with the bread crumbs and sprinkle on top of each shell. Bake in a preheated oven at 450 degrees until golden brown, about 7 to 10 minutes.

CHICKEN QUICHE

Serves 4

1 quiche pie shell
1 egg, separated, plus 3 egg
    yolks
1 cup cooked chicken, finely
    diced
1/2 cup cooked tongue or ham,
    finely diced

1/2 cup shredded Gruyère
    (optional)
Salt and white pepper
1/2 teaspoon dry mustard
1-1/2 cups light cream, a little
    more if needed, scalded

"Paint" the inside of the pie shell lightly with egg white and bake partially in a preheated oven at 350 degrees for 10 minutes.

Distribute the diced chicken, tongue, or ham and the optional cheese over the bottom of the pie shell. Whisk the 4 egg yolks with salt, pepper, and the mustard. Add the scalded cream in a thin stream and continue to whisk until well blended. Pour into the pie shell and if necessary add a little more cream.

Bake at 375 degrees until the quiche is done, about 30 minutes. The quiche will be done when a knife inserted in the center of the pie comes out clean.

TACOS DE GALLINA (CHICKEN TACOS)

Makes 12 tacos

Cooking oil

1 large onion, chopped

1 tablespoon all-purpose flour

1/2 cup broth or milk

3 tomatoes, peeled, seeded, and chopped

1 small avocado, chopped (optional)

1 chili pepper, chopped

1 teaspoon chili powder

3 cups chicken cubed, cooked

Salt to taste

12 tortillas, slightly warm

2 or 3 cups shredded lettuce

1 cup grated cheese

Taco sauce

Heat 1/4 cup cooking oil in a skillet and sauté the onion over low heat for about 10 minutes, stirring now and then. Add the flour and broth or milk, stirring. Add the tomatoes, avocado, chili peppers and powder, chicken, and salt to taste. Cook over low heat for 10 to 15 minutes or until the flour no longer tastes raw. Stir at times to avoid burning.

While the filling is cooking, heat about 1 inch of oil in a skillet. Fold one tortilla shell at a time loosely in half and quickly fry to a golden color, turning once to fry both sides evenly.

Place some of the filling in each shell. Add a little shredded lettuce, then some grated cheese. Top with a little taco sauce.

CHICKEN CROQUE MONSIEUR

The famous French cheese sandwich, chicken slices added.

For 1 sandwich

2 slices white bread
2 tablespoons softened butter
1 slice Swiss cheese

Dijon-type mustard
1 slice cooked ham
Slices of cooked chicken

Butter the bread lightly on both sides. Place the cheese on 1 of the slices and spread it with mustard. Add the ham and chicken and cover with the second slice of bread. Fry slowly in the remaining butter, turning once, until golden brown on both sides. Serve very hot.

CHICKEN CROQUETTES

Serves 4 or 5

1/2 cup chopped shallots or
   minced scallion bulbs
1 tablespoon butter
3 cups cooked chicken, finely
   chopped
1 cup ham, finely chopped
1 cup chopped fresh
   mushrooms

3 egg yolks
About 1 cup Sauce Velouté (see
   below)
Salt and pepper
1/4 cup milk
All-purpose flour
Bread crumbs
Cooking oil

Sauté the shallots or scallions in the butter until transparent, about 5 minutes; stir often and don't let them brown. Cool.

Combine the chicken, ham, mushrooms, and shallots or scallions.

Beat 2 of the egg yolks lightly and add to the cold Sauce Velouté. Season to taste.

Add enough of this sauce to the chicken mixture to hold shapes. Croquettes may be shaped in various ways, the most common one resembling a drumstick.

Beat the remaining egg yolk with the milk. Dip the croquettes first in flour, then in the egg mixture, and last in bread crumbs. Leave for 1 hour to dry at room temperature, or several hours in the refrigerator.

Heat 1 inch of cooking oil in a skillet and fry the croquettes, a few at a time, over medium to low heat until golden brown. Turn only once. Drain on paper towels and repeat until all the croquettes have been cooked.

SAUCE VELOUTÉ

1-1/2 tablespoons butter
1-1/2 tablespoons all-purpose
   flour

1-1/2 cups hot chicken or veal
   stock
Salt and white pepper

Melt the butter in a saucepan and add the flour. Stir with a wooden spoon and cook over low heat, without letting the roux brown, for 2 or 3 minutes. Remove from the heat and add the hot stock all at once, beating briskly with a whisk. Return the sauce to low heat and cook, stirring, until it is smooth and has thickened to the desired consistency. Season and cool completely before using in the above recipe.

CHICKEN FRITTERS

Serves 2

2 cups cooked noodles
1 cup diced, cooked chicken
Cooking oil
1 very small onion, finely
    chopped

2 eggs, beaten
Salt and pepper

In a mixing bowl combine the noodles and chicken. Heat a little oil in a skillet and sauté the onion, without browning, until transparent—about 7 minutes. Stir often. Transfer the onions with a slotted spoon to the noodle mixture. Add the eggs and seasoning. Leave for 30 minutes to rest.

Add a little more oil to the skillet and fry the noodle mixture, a large tablespoon at a time, until the fritters are golden brown on both sides. Drain on paper towels and serve very hot.

THE VERSATILE CHICKEN LOAF

This rice- and pine nut-flavored loaf can be eaten hot or then cooled and fried in slices.

Serves 4 to 6

1-1/3 cups raw rice
About 3 cups chicken stock or
    soup
4 cups cooked chicken, diced

1 cup pine nuts
1 cup chopped onions
1-1/2 tablespoons salt, pepper,
    and garlic powder

Put into an electric blender half the rice and 1 cup of stock. Blend until the rice is pulverized. Strain this liquid into a heavy saucepan and repeat with the remaining rice. Cook the rice mixture over low to medium heat, stirring constantly. Add remaining chicken stock or soup as necessary to make a very thick smooth sauce. Add the remaining ingredients and simmer for 5 minutes for flavors to blend.

Pour the mixture into a well-greased loaf pan and cover first with wax paper and then with aluminum foil. Place in a pan of hot water in a 350-degree oven and bake for 30 minutes. Serve hot or allow to cool and refrigerate overnight. Next day unmold the loaf and cut into slices. Slip a piece of foil between each slice and wrap the sliced loaf for freezing. Take slices when and as needed, dust with flour, and fry in cooking oil until hot and golden on both sides.

CHICKEN SLAW

A little chili sauce adds spice to this shredded salad of chicken, tongue, and greens.

Serves 4

1/3 cup red wine vinegar
2/3 cup salad oil
Salt and freshly ground black
  pepper
3 tablespoons chili sauce
1 cup chopped watercress

2 cups finely shredded cabbage
1 cup cold, cooked tongue,
  julienne cut
2 cups cold, cooked chicken,
  julienne cut

Combine the vinegar, oil, salt, pepper, and chili sauce and reserve at room temperature.

In a salad bowl combine the watercress, cabbage, tongue, and chicken and toss with the reserved dressing—as much as suits your taste.

CHICKEN SALAD

Since the beets turn this salad a pretty pink, hard-boiled eggs cut in wedges make a pleasing decoration.

Serves 4 to 6

1 cup cole slaw, drained
3 cups cooked chicken, in
   bite-sized pieces
1 cup cooked peas
1 cup cooked celery root,
   julienne cut,
     OR 1 cup diced, cooked
     potatoes
1 cup diced, cooked beets

1 large dill pickle, chopped
1 medium-sized onion, minced
1 tablespoon capers, with some
   of their liquid
1 tablespoon Dijon-type
   mustard
1 cup mayonnaise
Salt and pepper to taste

Mix all the ingredients, adding a little horseradish if you'd like it even zestier.

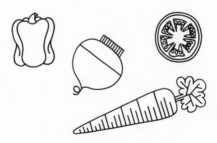

CHICKEN SALAD NIÇOISE

The famous Provençal salad—a beautiful arrangement of garden vegetables and chicken tossed first in vinaigrette.

Serves 8

3/4 cup salad oil
1/4 cup tarragon vinegar
2 cloves garlic, peeled and crushed
Salt and lemon pepper or pepper
1 pound fresh green beans, cooked and kept hot
1 or 2 small heads Boston lettuce
3 large tomatoes, peeled and sliced thick
1 red onion, sliced and separated into rings

The cubed meat from a 5- to 6-pound poached chicken (see pages 5-6)
2 tablespoons capers
4 hard-boiled eggs, quartered
1 bunch red radishes, trimmed and washed
16 large black olives
16 anchovies
1 bunch small scallions

In a large salad bowl combine the oil, vinegar, garlic, salt and pepper; whisk to blend. Add the hot cooked beans to the dressing and toss well. Allow them to cool in the dressing.

Arrange the lettuce leaves around the rim of a large platter. Remove the beans from the dressing with a slotted spoon, shaking off as much excess dressing as possible. Arrange as a bed inside the lettuce border on the platter. Add the tomato slices to the dressing, toss, then arrange them over the beans. Cover with onion rings. Add the chicken and capers to the dressing, toss, then place on top of the onion rings. Place the eggs in a circle around the chicken on the lettuce. Garnish the top of the salad with the radishes, olives, anchovies, and scallions. Serve slightly chilled.

THREE-CHEESE CHICKEN PIE

A magnificently rich pie made of sausage, chicken, ricotta, mozzarella, and Parmesan—to be served cold.

Serves 8 to 10

THE CRUST

2-1/2 cups instant-blending flour
1 teaspoon salt
1 tablespoon baking powder

1 tablespoon granulated sugar
1 stick (1/4 pound) butter
2 eggs

THE FILLING

1 to 1-1/2 pounds Polish sausage, sliced
2 fryers, poached (see pages 5-6)
2 pounds ricotta
4 eggs

2 or 3 cloves garlic, peeled and crushed
1/2 pound mozzarella, cubed
6 to 8 whole scallions, chopped
Salt and pepper or paprika
1/3 cup grated Parmesan

First make the crust. Combine the dry ingredients in a bowl. Cut the butter into the flour mixture, then work with your fingers until the mixture becomes crumbly. Add the eggs and work into a dough. Let the dough rest, well covered, at room temperature for 15 minutes. Roll out and line a rectangular or oval pan, about 12 by 9 by 2 inches.

Line the bottom of the pie crust with the sliced sausage. Take the meat off the chicken in fairly large pieces and place almost all of it on top of the sausages. Season lightly.

Beat the ricotta, eggs, and garlic with a whisk till well blended. Stir in the mozzarella and chopped scallions, then season with salt and some pepper or paprika. Spread this mixture over the chicken. Sprinkle the Parmesan on top and bake in a preheated oven at 400 degrees for 40 minutes, or until the pie is golden brown and done. Serve cold.

CHICKEN MEAT LOAF

This is good hot or cold.

Serves 6 to 8

1 small onion, chopped
1 clove garlic, peeled
2 eggs
3 tablespoons Dijon-type
  mustard
1 tablespoon salt
1/4 teaspoon cracked pepper

3 drops Tabasco sauce
1 chicken, cooked, boned, and
  diced
2 pounds lean ground beef
1 cup grated Cheddar
  cheese
Bread crumbs

In an electric blender combine the first 7 ingredients and blend until smooth.

In a large bowl combine the sauce with all the other ingredients except the bread crumbs. Mix well and shape the mixture like a large sausage. Spread the bread crumbs on a piece of aluminum foil a little larger than the chicken loaf.

Roll the chicken loaf in the bread crumbs until it is completely coated. Discard excess crumbs and wrap the loaf in the aluminum foil. Place in a baking pan and bake in a preheated oven at 400 degrees for 30 minutes. Cut the foil open and peel back as much as possible to allow the meat to brown. Continue to cook until done and crisp, about 20 minutes. Serve hot or cold in slices.

The Other Good Parts

LIVERS, GIBLETS, WINGS

And then there are times when you want those often-neglected delicacies—the chicken livers, giblets, or wings. Here are some good, earthy recipes such as Chicken Livers with Corn or Spanish-Style Chicken Wings, and a few sumptuous ones, such as Emilie's Speedy Pâté or Carolyn's Livers in Aspic.

And when you're alone or maybe with one other person, and you're cooking a chicken and don't need or want to save the liver and giblets: heat some butter in a small skillet, add first the chopped giblets and sauté them, turning often, till they're crisp and brown, then put in the chopped liver and sauté till brown but not hard. Drain briefly on paper towels, sprinkle them with a little salt, and eat them with a little cold butter.

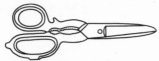

CHICKEN LIVERS, HOT

CHICKEN LIVER RAGOÛT

A lovely wine, mushroom, and mustard sauce coats the chicken livers. The ragoût would go beautifully with rice.

Serves 2 or 3

2 tablespoons chopped shallots	1/2 cup water
2 tablespoons butter	1 cup dry red wine
1 cup sliced fresh mushrooms	1 tablespoon mustard sauce or
1 pound chicken livers, cut in	mild mustard
half	Salt and freshly ground pepper

Sauté the shallots in butter over very low heat, stirring, until they are fully cooked and a rich brown—about 15 minutes. Add the mushrooms and sauté until brown—about 3 to 5 minutes. Add the chicken livers and cook over high heat until they are brown outside and pink inside. Transfer the livers to a plate and keep warm. Deglaze the pan, stirring and scraping, with the 1/2 cup water. Add the wine, mustard sauce, salt, and pepper and boil the sauce a minute or two. Return the livers to the pan and turn them in the foaming sauce only long enough to heat them thoroughly.

CHICKEN LIVER RAGOÛT WITH POACHED EGGS

Follow the recipe above. The eggs are poached right in the sauce. It is important for the sauce to be at the boiling point before each egg is added. Simmer only long enough for the eggs to "set."

CHICKEN LIVERS WITH CORN

A crisp sauté mixture on a bed of hot corn.

Serves 2

3 slices bacon, chopped
1 pound chicken livers, halved
4 shallots, chopped, or 1/4 cup scallions, chopped
2 tablespoons brandy

Salt and pepper
Water or stock, if necessary
2 servings of cooked corn kernels, hot

Sauté the bacon pieces until almost crisp. Add the livers and cook quickly to a golden brown. Remove them with a slotted spoon and reserve. Add the shallots or scallions to the skillet and sauté slowly to a golden brown, stirring often. Return the livers to the skillet and add the brandy. Scrape to incorporate all particles from the bottom of the skillet, adding a little water or stock if necessary. Season and serve on a bed of corn.

LIVER, SAUSAGE, AND RICE CASSEROLE

A wonderfully rich combination, topped with cheese.

Serves 6

2 tablespoons chicken fat or cooking oil
1 pound chicken livers, cleaned
1 pound Polish or garlic sausage, sliced
2 medium-sized onions, finely chopped
2 cloves garlic, minced
1 cup sliced fresh mushrooms
2 cups raw rice

4 cups boiling chicken stock or boiling water to which a chicken bouillon cube has been added
A good pinch saffron
1 tablespoon salt
1 package frozen peas, thawed
1/2 cup grated Parmesan
A few pats butter

Heat the chicken fat or oil in a skillet; add and brown the chicken livers. Remove with a slotted spoon and reserve. Add the sausage and brown lightly. Remove with a slotted spoon, drain on paper towels, and reserve with the chicken livers. Add the onions to the fat or oil in the skillet and cook slowly for about 5 minutes, stirring often. Add the garlic and mushrooms and cook for 5 minutes more, stirring often. Add the rice and stir until the rice is well coated with fat. Transfer this mixture to a casserole and add the boiling liquid, saffron, and salt. Bring to a boil on top of the stove. Then cover, turn heat very low, and cook as slowly as possible for 20 minutes.

Meanwhile, preheat oven to 425 degrees.

Add the reserved chicken livers, sausage, peas, and most of the cheese and stir well with a fork. Top with the remaining cheese and a few pats of butter. Cover again and put the casserole in the hot oven until the ingredients are heated through and the cheese has melted, about 20 minutes.

CHICKEN LIVER MOUSSE IN BROTH

Serves 4

4 large chicken livers
3 eggs
1 tablespoon dry sherry
1 shallot, chopped

Salt and pepper
4 cups good chicken broth
Chopped parsley

In an electric blender combine the chicken livers, eggs, sherry, and the chopped shallot. Blend until very smooth. Butter 4 china egg coddlers, china ramekins, or any other small china molds. Divide the liver mixture among them and cover the molds. If necessary, shape covers out of double-thick aluminum foil. Place the covered molds in a pan of water that covers two-thirds of the molds. Simmer the liver mousse until firm, about 15 to 20 minutes. Turn each one out onto a soup plate and add hot broth. Decorate with chopped parsley.

CHICKEN LIVERS, COLD

EMILIE'S SPEEDY PÂTÉ

1 pound best Braunschweiger
    liverwurst
2 sticks (1/2 pound) unsalted
    butter
1/2 cup heavy cream
1/4 teaspoon grated nutmeg
1/8 teaspoon white pepper
1/2 cup port

1/4 cup Cognac
1 pound chicken livers, lightly
    sautéed in butter or chicken
    fat
1/2 teaspoon anchovy paste
Pinch of ground cardamom
Aspic (see below)

Combine all the ingredients, except the aspic, in an electric blender and blend until perfectly smooth. The resulting pâté may be put in a large mold lined with aspic or into small, individual molds and be turned out. Or it can be put in ramekins with a thin layer of decorated aspic over the top.

ASPIC

Aspic is made by adding 1 teaspoon brandy and 1 teaspoon gelatin to 1 can of good consommé.

CHOPPED CHICKEN LIVERS

A little brandy gives the final flavor to this cold minced mixture.

1 medium-sized onion, finely
  chopped
3 tablespoons chicken fat
1 pound chicken livers

2 hard-boiled eggs
1 teaspoon salt
Pepper to taste
2 tablespoons brandy

Sauté half of the chopped onions in chicken fat until transparent; set aside the other half. Add the chicken livers and cook slowly, stirring frequently, for about 10 minutes (do not brown). Remove the livers from the pan and set aside the drippings. Chop the livers and hard-boiled eggs finely and combine them. Add the remaining raw, chopped onion, drippings from the pan, salt, pepper, and brandy. Mix well and chill.

CHICKEN LIVERS WITH FRESH GINGER

Traditional Chinese flavorings are used in this cold dish. Multiply as you wish, but even with a pound or so of livers, don't use more than 3 tablespoons peanut oil.

Serves 1

1 tablespoon peanut oil
A few drops sesame oil
1/2 tablespoon fresh ginger
    root, minced
2 or 3 chicken livers, halved

1 tablespoon chopped scallion
    bulbs
2 tablespoons dry sherry
1 tablespoon soy sauce

Combine the peanut and sesame oil and sauté the ginger, without browning, for 1 or 2 minutes. Remove with a slotted spoon and reserve. Sauté the livers in the same oil until golden brown and done the way you like them. Remove with a slotted spoon.

In a small bowl combine the livers, ginger, scallions, sherry, and soy sauce. Chill and serve cold.

CAROLYN'S LIVERS IN ASPIC

Serves 12

1 envelope unflavored gelatin
2 cups cold brown beef stock or
    bouillon made of cubes
The juice of 1/2 lemon
3/4 pound chicken livers
1/2 small onion, chopped

2 eggs, separated, plus 2 egg
    yolks
2 cups heavy cream
Salt and freshly ground pepper
1 teaspoon ground allspice
2 tablespoons minced parsley

Soak the gelatin in a small amount of the cold beef stock. Heat the remaining stock. Remove from the heat and stir in the softened gelatin and lemon juice. Cool.

Combine the chicken livers, onion, and 4 egg yolks in an electric blender. Blend until smooth and put the mixture in a bowl. Stir in the cream, salt, pepper, allspice, and parsley. Beat the egg whites until firm and fold into the liver mixture. Pour half the gelatin mixture into a well-oiled loaf pan and chill; reserve the other half at room temperature. Pour the liver mixture into a second well-oiled loaf pan. Bake in a pan of water in a preheated oven at 350 degrees for 1 hour. Cool completely. When cold, transfer into the pan containing the set aspic and cover with the remaining aspic. Chill overnight.

GIBLETS

CHICKEN GIBLETS PAPRIKAS

The giblets are simmered till tender, then combined with a paprika-sour cream sauce. This would be very good with rice.

Serves 4

2 pounds chicken giblets, cleaned

1 medium-sized onion, peeled and halved

2 carrots, halved

2 stalks celery, halved

4 sprigs parsley

1 clove garlic, peeled and halved

Water to cover (at least 4 cups)

Salt and pepper

4 slices bacon, cut into 1-inch pieces

2 large onions, finely chopped

1 green pepper, seeded and chopped

1 large or 2 small tomatoes, peeled, seeded, and chopped

2 tablespoons sweet Hungarian paprika

1 cup sour cream

3 egg yolks, beaten

Combine the giblets, halved onion, carrots, celery, parsley, garlic, and salt and pepper in a heavy casserole with water to cover and bring to a boil over low heat. Cover and simmer for 1 hour or more, until the giblets are tender. Skim if necessary. Strain the liquid, reserving the giblets and discarding the other solids. Boil the liquid to reduce to about 2 cups. Reserve.

Cook the bacon pieces until they're crisp. Add the chopped onions and sauté for about 10 minutes over medium heat, stirring often. Add the green pepper and cook 10 minutes longer. Add the tomatoes, paprika, and reserved giblets and stir. Add the reserved liquid and simmer for at least 10 minutes for flavors to blend.

Combine the sour cream and beaten egg yolks. Add the giblet mixture to the sour cream, stir, correct the seasoning, and serve at once.

WINGS

CHINESE CHICKEN WINGS

Serves 2

6 to 8 chicken wings
1 cup water
1/4 cup soy sauce
1/4 cup ginger wine

1 teaspoon minced fresh ginger
    root
1/4 teaspoon hot bean paste
    OR 1 hot Chinese pepper

Chop the chicken wings at the joints; discarding the bony tips is optional. Place all the ingredients in a heavy saucepan and simmer, covered, until the chicken wings are almost done. Uncover and boil rapidly, stirring constantly, until almost all the liquid has evaporated. The sauce that is left should now be thick and only enough to cover the wings well.

SPANISH-STYLE CHICKEN WINGS

Chicken wings are baked with rice in saffron-flavored stock. A beautiful, bright-yellow dish.

Serves 4 to 6

2 large pork chops, boned and
   diced
2 tablespoons cooking oil
12 chicken wings

1-1/2 cups raw rice
3 cups chicken stock
1 tablespoon salt
1/8 teaspoon saffron

Heat the oil in a skillet and brown the diced pork. Remove with a slotted spoon, drain, and reserve. Add the chicken wings to the skillet, a few at a time, and brown on all sides. Transfer the meat, wings, and pan drippings to a large casserole. Add the rice.

Heat the chicken stock and add salt and saffron to it. Bring to a boil and pour over the rice and wings. Cover the casserole well and bake in a preheated oven at 350 degrees until the wings are cooked, about 1-1/4 hours.

Index